WITNESSES OF PERFECT LOVE

WITNESSES OF PERFECT LOVE

NARRATIVES OF CHRISTIAN PERFECTION IN EARLY METHODISM

AMY CASWELL BRATTON

Clements Academic
Toronto

Copyright © 2014 by Amy Caswell Bratton

All rights reserved. No part of this book may be reproduced, stored in a retrieval system or transmitted in any form or by any means without the prior written permission from the publisher, or, in the case of photocopying or other reprographic copying, permission from Access Copyright, 1 Yonge Street, Suite 1900, Toronto, Ontario M5E 1E5 Canada.

Clements Publishing Group Inc.
6021 Yonge Street, Box 213
Toronto, Ontario M2M 3W2 Canada
www.clementspublishing.com

Library and Archives Canada Cataloguing in Publication

Bratton, Amy Caswell, 1980-, author
Witnesses of perfect love : narratives of Christian perfection in early Methodism / Amy Caswell Bratton.

(Tyndale studies in Wesleyan theology and history ; vol. 4)

Includes bibliographical references.
Issued in print and electronic formats.
ISBN 978-1-926798-44-8 (bound).–ISBN 978-1-926798-30-1 (pbk.).–
ISBN 978-1-926798-42-4 (html).–ISBN 978-1-926798-43-1 (pdf)

1. Perfection—Religious aspects—Methodist Church—History of doctrines—18th century. 2. Methodist Church—Doctrines—History—18th century. I. Title. II. Series: Tyndale studies in Wesleyan history and theology ; v. 4

BT766.B73 2014   234'.8

C2014-901347-7
C2014-901348-5

Contents

Foreword		vii
Acknowledgements		ix
Introduction		1

Part I. NARRATIVES OF PERFECTION: Setting the Stage

1.	Early British Methodism and the History of Christian Perfection	7
2.	Theological Context: The teaching of the Wesleys	15
3.	The Language of Perfection Narratives	29
4.	Narrative as a Sources for Theology	35
5.	The Power of Perfection Narratives	41

Part II. NARRATIVES OF PERFECTION: Four Early Methodists

6.	Sarah Crosby and Longing for Perfection	49
7.	George Clark and the Transformed Life	65
8.	William Hunter Preaching Christian Perfection	81
9.	Bathsheba Hall and Growth in Grace	95
10.	The Elements of Perfection Narratives	111

Conclusion	119
The Sources	127
Bibliography	131

Foreword

It is hard to argue with someone's own experience.

Whatever one may think of the doctrine of Christian perfection, hearing people relate what they have actually felt and seen in their own lives may cause a skeptical person to give the teaching a second look.

John Wesley famously wrote that the doctrine of Christian perfection was "the grand depositum which God has lodged with the people called Methodists; and for the sake of propagating this chiefly He appeared to have raised us up." Wesley based this conclusion in large measure on the actual fruit he saw in the lives of many of the early Methodists.

In spiritual matters, people may and often do make extravagant claims. Their behavior may betray their claims. No one was more aware of this than John Wesley himself. Nevertheless, when a parade of witnesses relates in simplicity and sincerity how God has transformed their lives and is working in and through them, and when a surrounding community confirms the authenticity of the witness, we sit up and take notice.

Amy Caswell Bratton's study of early Methodist perfection narratives is a timely and welcome contribution to our understanding of now Christian perfection actually "worked" in early Methodism. It also speaks to the ongoing relevance of personal spiritual experience in the church's life and mission today. Stories and personal experience spark interest not only in the eighteenth-century age of reason and revival but also in the twenty-first-century age of postmodernism and all kinds of spiritual experimentation.

Granted, the narratives analyzed here, like all such accounts, are shaped partly by the language and images of the time — in this case, the dynamic emerging culture of early Methodism. Such narratives tend to fit a pattern, as the author notes. That however is true of virtually all narratives in all times. We are helped by understanding the cultural, theological, and communal context of personal narratives. This book does provides such understanding.

Historically, Methodism has produced many theological and historical studies of Wesleyan Christian perfection, or perfect love. It has not however had enough studies like this one, which fill in the personal details, the actual stories, of the primal witnesses to what early Methodists actually experienced. This volume is thus a welcome addition to the literature of the Wesleys and their movement in its most dynamic days.

Bratton's main argument is that in early Methodism "the doctrine of Perfection passed from person to person through narrative." She documents how this actually occurred and emphasizes the importance of this for the church today. As she puts it, "theological claims made through narrative must be supported by an appealing faith-filled life." Narrative becomes powerful when it is "paired with the transformed lives to which the narratives witness."

Wesleyan theology and early Methodism still have much to teach the worldwide universal church, in both doctrine and experience. We are pleased therefore to add this book as the fourth volume in the Tyndale Series in Wesleyan History and Theology.

Howard A. Snyder
Chair of Wesley Studies, Tyndale Seminary (2007-2012)

Acknowledgements

I am deeply indebted to a wide variety of people; this project truly was a community endeavor. Thank you to friends, family and fellow Regent College students who talked with me as I wrestled through the meaning of early Methodist spirituality. Thank you to my fellow Regent student and Wesleyan scholar, Lucas Endicott, for many conversations about Wesley and Methodism. Thank you to Dr. Howard Snyder and Dr. David Hempton for taking the time to meet with me and discuss my ideas early in the project; you both encouraged me to focus on the people and their narratives and for this wise guidance I am deeply grateful.

Thank you to my fellow participants in the Summer Wesley seminar at Duke Divinity School in 2009. I would like to particularly thank Dr. Randy Maddox and Dr. Richard Heitzenrater for your suggestions, questions and direction toward resources. My research is immeasurably richer for having had the opportunity to use the resources of Duke Divinity School during this seminar.

I am also grateful to have had the opportunity to present portions of this project at various conferences. The *2009 Lilly Fellows Research Conference* "The Pietist Impulse in Christianity," March 19-21, 2009 at Bethel University; the *First Annual Regent College Student Association Academic Symposium 2009* and *The Conference on Faith & History* at George Fox University, October 7-9, 2010. I am particularly grateful to Dr. Howard Snyder and the *Second Annual Wesley Symposium* at Tyndale College (March 23, 2010) for allowing me to present a portion of this work. Your warm support for my research and faith-filled engagement with the topic was a great encouragement. I have been extremely blessed by the opportunity to publish my research in the Tyndale series on Wesleyan History and Theology, an opportunity which developed out of the 2010 Symposium.

Thank you to Dr. Gordon T. Smith who acted as my advisor for the early stages of this work at Regent College, and thank you to my supervisor for the remainder of the project, Dr. D. Bruce Hindmarsh. Thank you, Bruce, for your expert insight and for always challenging me to make this project the best that it can be. It was always a joy to share these ideas with a kindred spirit who engaged them with the rigor of a historian and the tender heart of a mystic.

Thank you to my gracious friends and proof-readers: Jennifer McClung, Lydia Cruttwell, Marie Morrison, Sarah Chestnut, Amy Crawford and Johannah Wetzel. Thank you for your eye for detail and your affirmation throughout my revisions.

Thank you to my family for your love and support over the years of study at Regent. It has been a great blessing to know that you support my passion for Christian spirituality and my calling to study and teach. Last, but certainly not least, thank you to my husband, Tim, for all your support and encouragement, your good questions and the continual reminder that this work is relevant to real life. Thank you for being so gracious whenever this project appeared to overwhelm me; you are an anchor in my life. I have been working on this project longer than I have known Tim, and when some of our first conversations surrounded my thesis topic he engaged my ideas with joy and curiosity. That is when I began to learn that Tim was someone with whom I wanted to continue to share my research, and my life.

Introduction

This morning I thought much of the descent of the Holy Ghost on the Apostles, and prayed that He might rest upon me. But I found little answer till the singing of the first hymn, when his Spirit made me deeply sensible of his presence. I then pleaded with him, and that with many tears, to make me a partaker of his sanctifying love, by removing forever the bitter root of pride, self-will and unbelief. All this time my heart was broken before the Lord, and my face covered with tears: and I found nothing left but a fear lest the Spirit should depart, before he had purified me from inbred sin. While I was thus agonizing with God in prayer, the power of the Lord came upon me, so that my whole body trembled under it. But I kept my spirit still, and continually cried, "My heart, Lord! work within! work within!" In that instant I felt the Spirit of God enter into my heart with mighty power, and as it were literally accomplish that promise, *I will take away the heart of stone, and give you a heart of flesh*: the old heart seeming to be taken away, and God himself taking possession of my soul in the fulness of love: and all the time of the service, I enjoyed such a heaven of love as I never before experienced. All the day I watched every motion of my heart, to see if the evils I before felt were there or not: but I found none: I could find nothing there, but solid joy and heart-felt peace.

- George Clark, Pentecost Sunday, 1762[1]

This fascinating journal entry bears witness to the spiritual experience of a Methodist man in London in the eighteenth century. It shows how George Clark prayed for God's presence in his life, and he was made aware of his sins of pride and self-will. Then in response to his plea, Clark encountered God in an intimate way which left him feeling cleansed from his sins and at peace. His account is just one of many spiritual narratives from this period which document the experience of Christian Perfection.

In the eighteenth century, narratives of spiritual experiences were circulating among British Methodists to express what God had done in their lives. Narratives of Christian Perfection conveyed an experience that could not

---

1. George Clark, "An Extract from the Journal of Mr. G— C—," in *Arminian Magazine*, 6 (1783), 244-245.

fully be explained using theological arguments about the doctrine. This book examines how the idea of Christian Perfection was transmitted through the use of story. Furthermore, it explores the content which was transmitted — that is the specific expression of Christian maturity as seen in the Wesleyan Methodist doctrine of Christian Perfection.

I will argue that the doctrine of Christian Perfection, while defined and taught by key leaders such as John and Charles Wesley, was significantly spread among the early Methodist communities by narratives that embodied the doctrine, bearing witness to an experience of God's love, as well as holiness of life, thus inspiring believers to seek out their own experience of Christian Perfection. I will illustrate this argument through the examination of first-hand narratives of the experience of Christian Perfection written by early Methodists in Britain and published for the edification of the community.[2]

This book is primarily the work I completed for my Master's thesis at Regent College. I did not set out to write on narrative, or even about the lesser known early Methodist people. I began with questions about the Methodist doctrine of Christian Perfection. Questions about what exactly John Wesley taught, and why his teaching seemed so foreign today, even in churches who claim the Wesleyan tradition. As I began to read the theology and history summarized in the following chapters I became more confused. Wesley said many things, in many different context over several decades about the doctrine of Christian Perfection, and his comments do not appear to be consistent. There must be more going on during this time period than I was grasping. Then one question led me out of the fog. If Wesley himself did not claim to have experienced Christian Perfection, did anyone else claim the experience? What do they have to say about the experience, rather than the theology? This question led me to the narrative of William Hunter found in chapter eight, then his intriguing story led me to seek out others. I fully intended to address my original questions, but as I dug deeper and talked to others about what I was finding (or rather the people I was discovering) it became clear that the stories of early Methodist Perfection were central to understanding the ideas. The people who held to these beliefs were essential to understanding the theology. I see now that my attempt to take the idea of Christian Perfection out of its eighteenth-century context (the narratives of those who experienced Perfection) led to my confusion when faced with Wesley's theology alone.

---

2. This study will examine only published sources of Perfection narratives, but one can imagine that comparing manuscript sources of edited material (if it could be located) would produce an even richer collection of stories.

The doctrine of Christian Perfection has always been controversial, and John Wesley was particularly protective of those who he deemed to be genuine professors of an experience of Christian Perfection. The title of this book, comes from a journal entry by Sarah Crosby on May 1, 1774, noting this attitude in Wesley. She writes, "He told the Society, that whosoever spake against *those who were simple witnesses of perfect love*, spake against those, who were as *dear to him* as the *apple of his eye*."[3]

The four central accounts in this book were selected for their first-hand story of an experience of the instantaneous event of Christian Perfection. These four complement each other because among them are men and women, lay preachers and non-preaching lay leaders; they are Sarah Crosby (1729–1804), George Clark (1710–1797), William Hunter (1728–1797) and Bathsheba Hall (1745–1780).

Before we get to the narratives, five introductory chapters will address Methodist history, Wesleyan theology, and narrative theology to provide context for the narratives that follow. In addition, I will explore the definition of Perfection through the words of the early Methodists themselves. Thus, chapter one will look chronologically at Methodism in the eighteenth century and then specifically at key events in the development of the doctrine of Perfection. In chapter two, the teaching of the key leaders John and Charles Wesley will provide theological context for the narratives. In chapter three, a survey of the language that was used by Methodist people in narratives of Christian Perfection will enrich the definition of Perfection offered by the leaders. Chapter four will explore narrative theology and lay the foundation for making observation about theology from narrative. Finally, chapter five will introduce my argument through a selection of stories to illustrate that the transmission of Christian Perfection took place through the medium of narrative.

Following the introductory chapters are four Methodist narratives which offer a sampling to examine both the historical spread of the idea of Perfection through narrative as well as the doctrine of Christian Perfection itself. The four narratives selected include men and women, lay preachers and local leaders. Mrs. Sarah Crosby was a local leader in the Leeds area who answered the call to preach. Mr. George Clark was a local leader in London. Mr. William Hunter was a travelling lay preacher, preaching mainly in the North of England.

---

3. Sarah Crosby, *Biographical Sketches of the Lives and Public Ministry of Various Holy Women, whose eminent usefulness and successful labours in the Church of Christ, have entitled them to be enrolled among the great benefactors of mankind: In which are included several letters from the Rev. J. Wesley never before published*, ed. Z. Taft (London, 1825), 2:65. Emphasis in original.

Finally, Mrs. Bathsheba Hall was a local leader in Bristol. These four are a small sample, as the scope of this project does not allow for a comprehensive sampling of Perfection narratives.[4] These four offer merely a taste of the Wesleyan Methodist spirituality in eighteenth-century Britain by examining their narratives of Christian Perfection.

---

4. There are hundreds of published and manuscript Perfection narratives. Thomas Albin studied 555 early Methodist narratives, and found 245 that contained a sanctification narrative. Thomas R. Albin, "An Empirical Study of Early Methodist Spirituality," in *Wesleyan Theology Today: A Bicentennial Theological Consultation*, ed. Theodore Runyon (Nashville: Kingswood Books, 1985), 279.

PART I

NARRATIVES OF PERFECTION:
Setting the Stage

1

Early British Methodism and the History of Christian Perfection

> [The doctrine of Perfection] is the grand depositum which God has lodged with the people called Methodists; and for the sake of propagating this chiefly He appeared to have raised us up.
> — John Wesley to Robert Carr Brackenbury, 1790[1]

British Methodism in the Eighteenth Century

The Protestant tradition of Methodism traces its roots to revival activities connected to John and Charles Wesley in the eighteenth century. Methodism has spread world-wide and continues to grow and change, as well as retain distinctive elements that developed during its early history. One such distinctive element of Methodism is the doctrine of Christian Perfection. This doctrine is largely unknown or misunderstood in the Wesleyan churches, and in Protestantism more broadly. Yet, the doctrine of Christian Perfection, as understood in eighteenth-century England offers a significant contribution to the Christian understanding of discipleship and growth in Christian maturity, which are topics of great interest in the church today.

The historical scope of investigation for this study will focus on early British Methodism. Early Methodism can be defined by the influence and lifetime of John Wesley (1703-1791). The longevity of Wesley's life means that the period called early Methodism is significant in length, allowing for many changes in the movement. Historian Richard Heitzenrater offers a periodization of early Methodism in his book *Wesley and the People Called Methodists* which provides a brief history of the Methodist movement in the eighteenth century.[2]

---

1. John Wesley to Robert Carr Brackenbury, Bristol, September 15, 1790, in *The Letters of the Rev. John Wesley, A.M.* ed. John Telford. (London: Epworth Press, 1931), 8:238.

2. Richard P. Heitzenrater, *Wesley and the People Called Methodists* (Nashville: Abingdon Press, 1995).

The Rise of Methodism (1725 – 1739):
when the foundational ideas are developed by the Wesleys.

The Revival Begins (1739 – 1744):
when preaching, conversions, and organization into societies marks the landscape.

Consolidation of the Movement (1744 – 1758):
when the organizational structures are being refined.

The Maturing of Methodism (1758 – 1775):
when struggles sharpen the character of Methodism.

Tensions and Transitions (1775 – 1791):
when the elderly John Wesley prepares the Methodism connexion for his inevitable death.

These various periods represent different joys and struggles in the Methodist movement, and the doctrine of Christian Perfection has a unique history that unfolds during each period. This periodization of early Methodism will continue to be referenced to provide context for the stories that follow.

To further narrow the focus, the Perfection narratives in the four central accounts in this book occurred in a sixteen year period, from 1753 through 1769, during what Heitzenrater calls 'the maturing phase of Methodism.' Which is also the same time as the increased occurrence of Perfection narratives, and the Perfectionist controversy in London in the 1760s.

Keeping in mind this study's historical limitation to early Methodism, we should remind ourselves that many current-day readers of eighteenth-century texts regarding Christian Perfection are influenced by the history of the doctrine since that time. The nineteenth-century holiness movement in North America, and pentecostalism (birthed from the holiness movement) in the twentieth century, each developed their own interpretation of the doctrine of Perfection which shifted the popular understanding of the term. This examination is focused on the early Methodist understanding of Christian Perfection in an attempt to reconstruct the historical terrain without the aid of today's hindsight of where the nineteenth and twentieth-century interpretations of the doctrine would lead. Therefore, the historical limitation of this study intentionally predates the significant theological shift in the doctrine seen in the nineteenth century.[3]

---

3. For more on the shift in Christian Perfection during the holiness movement, see Randy L. Maddox, "Reconnecting the Means to the End: A Wesleyan Prescription for the Holiness Movement," *Wesleyan Theological Journal* 33 no. 2 (1998): 29-66.

The History of Christian Perfection in Early Methodism

The story of early Methodist Christian Perfection starts at the beginning of the eighteenth century, during the rise of Methodism.[4] Before the revival began, before Charles and John Wesley's experiences of assurance, they were already teaching holiness publicly, and seeking it personally. Charles sought holiness through the structured discipline of the Holy Club during his time at Oxford, and John soon joined him. John Wesley's personal crusade for holiness is seen when he made a declaration giving his whole life to God in 1725.[5] In addition, Wesley preached his first sermon on the doctrine of Perfection, the "Circumcision of the Heart," on January 1, 1733 at St. Mary's at Oxford.[6] In this sermon the ideal of holiness is drawn out from the promises of Scripture. Thus, the biblical ideal of holiness was set as a foundation stone for the doctrine of Perfection.

The next episode in the history of Perfection is the events surrounding Charles and John Wesley's experiences of assurance of pardon in 1738. The providential encounter of John and Charles Wesley with Moravian-Christians informed their expectation of an assurance experience. John already longed for assurance of pardon, and the Moravians became teachers of his heart by affirming his expectation. Interestingly, a shift in Moravian teaching occurred around the time that the Wesleys encountered them. The new teaching included an expectation of sanctification in the instant of justification (experienced as assurance) which was reached by quietly waiting for an act of mercy by God.[7]

---

4. For a more extensive history of John Wesley's writing on Christian Perfection, see D. Marselle Moore, "Development in Wesley's Thought on Sanctification and Perfection," *Wesleyan Theological Journal* 2 no 2 (1985): 29-53.

5. John Wesley, *A Plain Account of Christian Perfection, as believed and taught by the Rev. Mr. John Wesley, from the year 1725 to the year 1777*, 6th ed., §2 (London, 1789), 3. Heitzenrater, *People Called Methodists*, 36.

6. Wesley preached "The Circumcision of the Heart" on January 1, 1733 using the occasion of the Feast of the Circumcision of Christ as his inspiration for the image of Circumcision for holiness. The collect for this occasion draws this connection. The sermon was later included as the first sermon in the second volume of Sermons on Several Occasions, editing it slightly to include a personal experience of salvation to his assertion of cleansing. Introduction to the sermon by Albert C. Outler in *Sermons I: 1-33, The Bicentennial Edition of The Works of John Wesley*, 1:398-400.

7. The shift in teaching that spread to various Moravian missions worldwide is documented by Frederick Dreyer in his book *The Genesis of Methodism* (Bethlehem: Lehigh University Press, 1999), 37-54. An example of the new Moravian teaching and the its implications can be found in the conversation between Moravian leader, Count Zinzendorf and Wesley documented by Wesley, where

As anticipated, Charles Wesley (and John a few days later) experienced the transformative assurance of pardon to which their Moravian brothers and sisters testified. Yet the accompanying sanctification was lacking. Instead of discarding either his desire for holiness or the experience of pardon, John Wesley detached the experience of justification from the experience of sanctification. He now saw that an experience of justification and sanctification could be separated by time in the spiritual lifespan of the believer.[8] In this development, it is seen how the ideal of holiness (discovered in his study of Scripture) is set alongside his experience of the transforming power of God's grace. The two essential elements of ideal and experience are now present in John Wesley's life which is foundational for his later defence of an experience of holiness.

The next episode in the history of Methodism is the outbreak of revival in England. Much has been said about the period of Methodism as the revival begins.[9] Spiritual awakening occurred and the crowds gathered in Methodist societies to find out how to flee the wrath of God. Conversion narratives from this period are numerous.[10]

Alongside conversion, Methodists were also seeking Perfection. Early in the revival, testimony arose about an experience beyond conversion; the feeling of being freed from sin (or being entirely sanctified) began to emerge. As early as May 1741, John and Charles Wesley each record in their journals the deathbed scene of faithful saints that include claims of being freed from all sin. The Wesleys interpreted these stories as possible experiences of Christian Perfection.[11] Interestingly, historian Thomas Albin notes the correlation of

---

Zinzendorf argues that "from the moment one is justified, he is entirely sanctified. Thereafter till death he is neither more holy nor less holy." John Wesley, *John Wesley*, ed. Albert C. Outler (New York: Oxford University Press, 1964), 367-372.

8. For a nuanced read of the famous events of May 1738, see Richard P. Heitzenrater, "Great Expectations: Aldersgate and the Evidences of Genuine Christianity," in *Aldersgate Reconsidered*, ed. Randy L. Maddox (Nashville: Kingswood, 1990), 49-91.

9. For example, see Henry D. Rack, "The Revivals: Methodists and Evangelicals, Churchmen and Dissenters (1738-1760)," in *Reasonable Enthusiast: John Wesley and the Rise of Methodism*, 3rd ed. (London: Epworth, 2002), 282-313. Heitzenrater, "The Revival Begins (1739-1744)," in *Wesley and the People Called Methodists* (Nashville: Abingdon, 1995), 97-146. David Hempton, *Methodism: Empire of the Spirit* (New Haven: Yale University Press, 2005).

10. For more on conversion narratives, see Bruce Hindmarsh, *The Evangelical Conversion Narrative: Spiritual Autobiography in Early Modern England* (Oxford: Oxford University Press, 2005); and Phyllis Mack, "'Out of the paw of the lion': first conversion," in *Heart Religion in the British Enlightenment: Gender and Emotion in Early Methodism* (Cambridge: Cambridge University Press, 2008), 60-82.

11. Charles reports the faithful death of sister Hooper on May 6, 1741 and from her expression of devotion to Christ he interprets, "this is that holiness, or absolution, or Christian Perfection!" Charles

these deathbed accounts with the first recorded meeting of the select society on May 20, 1741. The select society is a special gathering with the express purpose of seeking Christian Perfection.[12] These events show that some in the Methodist community were seeking Perfection even as the revival began.

Christian Perfection became more central to the Methodism movement as it began to consolidate starting in 1744. John Wesley organized groups to meet the spiritual needs he observed: as believers were awakened by revival preaching, they were placed in Methodist societies for encouragement toward justification.[13] As seen in the minutes from Wesley's meeting with his preachers on August 2, 1745, it did not take long for further growth to be encouraged. It was observed that the preaching no longer only focused on repentance, but also encouraged believers to press on to Perfection.[14]

During the phase of Methodism Maturing (1758–1775), controversy arose about Christian Perfection. The 1760s brought an increase in claims of the experience of Perfection, which in turn brought about the Perfectionist controversy in London. Stephen Gunter, in his book *The Limits of 'Love Divine'*, provides a historical reconstruction of the events in London through archival sources.[15] In London, controversy arose surrounding claims to Perfection as these claims grew more extravagant. Some claimed angelic Perfection, or the

---

Wesley, *The Manuscript Journal of the Reverend Charles Wesley, M.A.* ed. ST Kimbrough, Jr. and Kenneth G. C. Newport (Nashville: Kingswood Books, 2008) 1:304. John Wesley visited a very ill friend, Nancy Morris, and her testimony on May 15, 1741 of being cleansed prompted Wesley to discuss the possibility of being cleansed from all sin with Moravian, Peter Böhler the next day. John Wesley, May 15, 1741, *Journal and Diaries II: 1738-1743*, edited by W. Reginald Ward and Richard Heitzenrater, vol. 19 of *The Bicentennial Edition of The Works of John Wesley* (Nashville: Abingdon Press, 1990), 194-195.

12. Thomas R. Albin, "'Inwardly Persuaded': Religion of the Heart in Early British Methodism," in *"Heart Religion" in the Methodist Tradition and Related Movements*, ed. Richard B. Steele (Lanham, Maryland and London: Scarecrow Press, 2001), 39. John Wesley, *Journal and Diaries II*, 19:461.

13. For John Wesley's account of the emergence of the structured groups in Methodism, see John Wesley, "Plain Account of the People Called Methodist," in *The Methodist Societies: History Nature and Design*, ed. Rupert E. Davies, vol. 9 of *The Bicentennial Edition of The Works of John Wesley* (Nashville: Abingdon, 1989), 253-280.

14. Wesleyan Methodist Church Conference. *Minutes of several conversations, between the Rev. John Wesley, A.M. and the preachers in connection with him. Containing the form of discipline established among the preachers and people in the Methodist societies*, (Dublin, 1749), 13. Citation found in August 2, 1745, question 15.

15. W. Stephen Gunter, "The Danger of Perfectionism," in *The Limits of 'Love Divine'* (Nashville: Kingswood, 1989), 202-226. See also Charles H. Goodwin, "Setting Perfection too High: John Wesley's Changing Attitudes Toward the 'London Blessing'," *Methodist History* 36, no. 2 (January 1998): 86-96., Gareth Lloyd, "'A Cloud of Perfect Witnesses': John Wesley and the London Disturbances 1760-1763," *The Asbury Theological Journal*, vol. 56 no. 2 - vol. 57, no 1. (2001-2002): 117-136.

inability to sin after their Perfection experience. In addition, a group claiming Perfection withdrew from fellowship with the London Methodists. They asserted that those perfected could only be taught by others who also had the experience.[16] These excessive claims were connected to two preachers in particular, Thomas Maxfield and George Bell. The height of the controversy occurred when Bell publicly prophesied the end of the world would occur on February 28, 1763. These prophetic claims prompted Wesley to publicly reject Bell with clear statements that Bell was no longer connected to the Methodist fellowship.[17]

Wesley has been criticized for his slow response to the controversy, and Gunter interprets the events suggesting that Wesley took a risk by allowing the events to continue. Using the parable Jesus taught about the wheat and the tares (Matthew 13:24-30), Gunter suggests that Wesley took the risk of allowing Maxfield and Bell to continue their ministry for the sake of the positive outcomes that were evident alongside the excesses.[18] In hindsight, the risk did produce some increased revival activity in this period, but this gain was held alongside the result of long-lasting skepticism about the doctrine of Christian Perfection in the London Methodist societies.[19]

---

16. Clark, "Journal," *Arminian Magazine*, 6 (1783) 299. Compare this group to the group of professors of Perfection that John Wesley met with in 1760: "Fri. [January]18 [1760]. I desired those who believed they were saved from sin (sixteen or seventeen in number) to meet me at noon, to whom I gave such cautions and instructions as I judged needful. Nor did any of these pretend to be above man's teaching but received it with all thankfulness." Wesley, *Journal & Diaries IV*, 21:239.

17. John Wesley wrote a brief letter to the London Chronicle newspaper declaring publicly the split with Bell. It reads, "I take this opportunity of informing all whom it may concern (1) that Mr. Bell is not a member of our Society; (2) that I do not believe either the end of the world or any signal calamity will be on the 28th instant; and (3) that not one in fifty, perhaps not one in five hundred, of the people called Methodists believe any more than I do either this or any other of his prophecies." John Wesley to the Editor of the London Chronicle, February 9, 1763, in *The Letters of the Rev. John Wesley, A.M.* ed. John Telford. 8 vols. (London: Epworth Press, 1931), 4:202-203.

18. Gunter, *Love Divine*, 225. Wesley saw the good being done amidst the harm, he notes this in a letter to his brother Charles: John Wesley to Charles Wesley, London, December 23, 1762 in *Letter*, 4:199. In addition, John Wesley himself uses the image of the wheat and the tares to interpret the Perfectionist controversy in the *Plain Account of Christian Perfection* where Wesley notes that someone wrote a letter to encourage him drawing from this parable. Wesley, *Plain Account of Christian Perfection*, 6th ed., §21, 53. Interestingly, Wesley publishes accounts from both Maxfield and Bell two decades later in the *Arminian Magazine*. This could indicate support of their experiences or could simply be a refusal to deny the events of the controversy. Nevertheless, the testimonies do exist in a published form thanks to Wesley, *Arminian Magazine*, 3 (1780) 385-386, 674-676.

19. George Clark notes in his journal that the controversy caused all Perfection claims to be doubted, not only by critics, but also by Methodists. He laments the losses for God's work of holiness as a result.

During the final stage of early Methodism another controversy arose as the transition began in preparation for the death of the elderly John Wesley. Following the Perfectionist controversy and continuing into the 1770s, the doctrine of Perfection became a key distinctive of the Methodist movement. This period is marked by the Minutes Controversy (beginning in 1770), in which Wesleyan Methodists found themselves in a very public battle with the Calvinists. During this season the Wesleyan Methodists defined themselves using the doctrine of Perfection over against other theological positions.[20] In addition, in 1778, John Wesley began to publish the *Arminian Magazine*, and narratives of Perfection were prominent in the Wesleyan Methodist identity formed by this monthly publication.[21] Thus, the *Arminian Magazine* is a key source for published narratives of Christian Perfection.

In summary, the doctrine of Christian Perfection and narratives of the experience of Perfection emerged in early Methodism amidst both revival and controversy. These historical events provide the context for the narratives examined here. Inseparable from the events is the teaching of the Wesley brothers which provides an important foundation for early Methodist understanding of Perfection, the topic to which we now turn.

Clark, *Arminian Magazine*, 6 (1783), 302. See also Mr. G. Clark to John Wesley, London, July 29, 1774, in *Arminian Magazine*, 10 (1787)104. John Pawson wrote in 1796 that in London, especially among the older Methodists, the excesses of Bell's teaching still lingered in the skepticism toward the doctrine of Christian Perfection: MS letter cited in Gunter, *Love Divine*, 225-226. For more examples of skepticism beyond London, see Charles H. Goodwin, "Setting Perfection too High: John Wesley's Changing Attitudes Toward the 'London Blessing'," *Methodist History* 36, no. 2 (January 1998): 92.

20. In the debate with the Calvinists, Wesley called for holiness in response to antinomianism. Rack notes, "[Wesley's] perfectionism was his favourite antidote to [antinomianism] and equally a prime cause of offense to Calvinists." Rack, *Reasonable Enthusiast*, 450. Ironically, the Calvinists accused those who supported Christian Perfection of antinomianism for claiming perfection and allowing for infirmities. Idem., 457.

21. John Wesley was the editor of the *Arminian Magazine* from 1778 until his death. John Wesley, ed. *The Arminian Magazine: Consisting of Extracts and Original Treatises on Universal Redemption* (London, 1778-1791).

2

Theological Context: The teaching of the Wesleys

Dear Sir,
    As the Lord has made your instruction so great a blessing to my soul, I think it my duty to let you hear from me. What you said of being "settled in the pure love of God," was greatly blest to me. While you spoke to me, I saw the grace set before me, and my heart was drawn out to the Lord in prayer, with a constant waiting upon him for the blessing, till at the Love-feast in York, under your prayer, the Lord revealed himself with such a weight of love, that my bodily strength was all removed, by his glorious appearing.

Mrs. E. M—n to John Wesley, 1762[1]

The influence of John Wesley and his brother Charles on the Methodist people is undeniable. The above account of spiritual encounter is just one example of the influence of John Wesley. This brief survey of the teaching of the Wesleys regarding Christian Perfection provides the context for both the role of the Wesley brothers as leaders, as well as context for the theology they taught, a theology that was held in common by many of the Methodist people.

John Wesley's teaching on Christian Perfection

    John Wesley's teaching on Christian Perfection is extensive, and within the corpus of his theological writing, John Wesley does not appear altogether consistent on Perfection. For example, in his letters to some people he insisted on a simple definition of Perfection, while the definition for others was quite extensive.[2] To most he wrote with confidence about the doctrine, but to his

---

1. Mrs. E. M—n to John Wesley, Potto, April 14, 1762, in *Arminian Magazine*, 4 (1781) 444-445.

brother Charles, John confessed his own doubts about nuances of the doctrine.³ Historian Stephen Gunter names this fluctuating theology an "occasional theology," drawing attention to the fact that Wesley responded to a wide variety of occasions and his advice varied according to each situation.⁴

To better understand the variation in his teaching, John Wesley's thoughts on Christian Perfection can be broken down into two groups: the ideal and the experiential. Granted, this is a distinction imposed upon Wesley's teaching and the two categories often overlap. Nevertheless, examining them separately helps in organizing the vast body of comments offered by Wesley on the topic of Perfection.⁵

The ideal of Christian Perfection

Wesley's main argument for Christian Perfection is that it is a biblical concept.⁶ His 1733 sermon "The Circumcision of the Heart" and his 1741

---

2. For extended definitions, see John Wesley to an Irish Lady, Tullamore, June 27, 1769, in *Letters*, 5:139-141; and John Wesley to Joseph Benson, London, December 28, 1770, in *Letters*, 5:214-215. For an example of short, terse definitions: "I told you [Perfection] was love; the love of God and our neighbour; the image of God stamped on the heart; the life of God in the soul of man; the mind that was in Christ, enabling us to walk as Christ also walked." John Wesley to Lawrence Coughlan, August 27, 1768, in *Letters*, 5:102.

3. John Wesley to Charles Wesley, Whithaven, June 27, 1766, in *Letters*, 5:15-16. John Wesley to Charles Wesley, Stockton, July 9, 1766, in *Letters*, 5:20. John Wesley to Charles Wesley, London, February 12, 1767, in *Letters*, 5:41.

4. Gunter, *Love Divine*, 202. Wesley makes the claim in *A Plain Account of Christian Perfection* that his teaching on Christian Perfection remained constant from 1725. Wesley, *Plain Account of Christian Perfection*, §6, 6. Moore concedes that some aspects of Christian Perfection developed while others stayed constant. Moore, "Development" *Wesleyan Theological Journal*, 47. However, Gunter argues that perfection did not develop, instead Perfection was at the core of what developed around it. Gunter, *Love Divine*, 202.

5. The life and teaching of John Wesley has been the topic of theologians and historians for centuries. This brief summary does not assume a comprehensive treatment. For more on John Wesley's life and theology, see Rack, *Reasonable Enthusiast*. Gunter, *The Limits of 'Love Divine.'* Randy L. Maddox, *Responsible Grace: John Wesley's Practical Theology* (Nashville: Kingwood, 1994). Harald Lindström, *Wesley and Sanctification: A study in the doctrine of salvation* (London: Epworth, 1946). W. E. Sangster, *The Path to Perfection: An Examination and Restatement of John Wesley's Doctrine of Christian Perfection* (London: Epworth Press, 1957).

6. In one example of John Wesley arguing for the biblical root of the doctrine of Perfection, he says: "this perfection cannot be a delusion, unless the Bible be a delusion, too." John Wesley to Lawrence Coughlan, August 27, 1768, in *Letters*, 5:102. For an example of Scripture that uses "perfect," see Hebrews 6:1 (KJV): "Therefore leaving the principles of the doctrine of Christ, let us go on unto

sermon entitled "Christian Perfection" establish the ideal of Perfection as seen in Scripture.[7] For example, in "The Circumcision of the Heart," Wesley argues that God cleanses humanity of sin through the power and sacrifice of Jesus Christ. This cleansing from sin enables Christians to seek purity of heart as 1 John 3:3 declares.[8] Wesley describes the vision of purity in this way:

> It is [the Christian's] daily care, by the grace of God in Christ, and through the blood of the covenant, to purge the inmost recesses of his soul from the lusts that before possessed and defiled it: from uncleanness, and envy, and malice, and wrath, from every passion and temper that is "after the flesh", that either springs from or cherishes his native corruption.[9]

However, even such thorough cleansing is not the complete picture; Wesley adds that cleansing is for the sake of being filled with love for God. He describes the ideal as the undivided heart filled with love for God and neighbour.[10]

Additionally, Wesley's argument in his sermon "Christian Perfection" further explores this call to Scriptural holiness. He begins this sermon by stating what Christian Perfection is not: "Christian perfection therefore does not imply (as some men seem to have imagined) an exemption either from ignorance or mistake, or infirmities or temptations. Indeed, it is only another term for holiness."[11] Moving on to what Christian Perfection does involve, Wesley first includes a discussion on sin, defined in the narrow sense as: a willful transgression of a known law.[12]

---

perfection." The Greek word translated "perfect" in the Authorized Version, or King James Version that John Wesley would have been using, is more often translated "maturity" or "completion" in more recent translation, causing the language of Perfection to be less familiar today. Additionally, Tyson notes that while Wesleyan theology of Perfection is biblical, it is not Pauline, which is why it is can be unfamiliar to Protestant sensibilities shaped by the epistles of Paul. Tyson, *Charles Wesley*, 163.

7. John Wesley, "The Circumcision of the Heart," in *Sermons I:1-33*, ed. Albert C. Outler, vol. 1 of *The Bicentennial Edition of The Works of John Wesley* (Nashville: Abingdon, 1984), 398-414. John Wesley, "Christian Perfection," in *Sermons II: 34-70*, ed. Albert C. Outler, vol. 2 of *The Bicentennial Edition of The Works of John Wesley* (Nashville: Abingdon, 1985), 96-124. In *Plain Account of Christian Perfection*, Wesley comments on the 1733 sermon and defends its value thirty years later arguing that to contradict it would be to contradict Scripture. Wesley, *Plain Account of Christian Perfection*, 6th ed., §6, 6.

8. 1 John 3:3: "And every man that hath this hope in him purifieth himself, even as he is pure." (KJV)

9. Wesley, Sermon 17, "Circumcision," §I.10 in *Works*, 1:407.

10. Ibid., §I.11-12, 1:407-408.

11. Wesley, Sermon 40, "Christian Perfection," §I.9 in *Works*, 2:104.

12. For an example of Wesley's definition of sin, see John Wesley to Mrs. Bennis, Yarm, June 16, 1772, in *Letters*, 5:322.

Wesley sets forth that the ideal way of salvation is, first, for a person to be awakened to his or her sinfulness. Subsequently, there is assurance that sin — personal sin, not only sin in a universal sense — is forgiven in some way that can be sensed. Then following this assurance of forgiveness (or justification), outward sin (that behaviour which contradicts the character of God) is set aside. Because Wesley saw that this was not an easy task, the class meeting was established where the class leader (one who was further along in the journey) questioned their class members regularly about their godly behaviour.

Furthermore, Wesley recognized that sin is not limited to outward sin. His sermon "On Sin in Believers" addresses the continuing struggle.[13] It is from two sources that Wesley argues that sin remains after justification: from the biblical admonishments to Christians against their sin, and from the experience of believers. He describes this experience as

> an heart bent to backsliding, a natural tendency to evil, a proneness to depart from God, and cleave to the things of earth. [Believers] are daily sensible of sin remaining in their heart, pride, self-will, unbelief, and of sin cleaving to all they speak and do, even their best actions and holiest duties.[14]

The above describes *inward* sin (or *inbred* sin), a term used by Wesley. Fortunately, Wesley offers hope for release from this inbred sin, in addition to the release from outward sin experienced at conversion. His vision of holiness and Perfection is exactly that — release from inbred sin discovered by the believer after justification. Just as assurance of forgiveness marks conversion, an encounter with God experienced through the spiritual senses marks the purgation of inbred sin. This encounter is Christian Perfection.

In Wesley's sermon, "Christian Perfection" he frames the promises of Scripture for cleansing from sin in a vision of becoming Christ-like. He writes,

> [The Christian] is purified from pride; for Christ was lowly of heart. He is pure from self-will or desire; for Christ desired only to do the will of his Father, and to finish his work. And he is pure from anger, in the common sense of the word, for Christ was meek and gentle, patient and long suffering. ... Thus doth Jesus "save his people from their sins": and not only from outward sins, but also from the sins of their hearts; from evil thoughts and from evil tempers.[15]

---

13. Wesley, Sermon 13, "On Sin in Believers," in *Works*, 1:314-334.
14. Wesley, Sermon 13, "On Sin", §III.7 in *Works*, 1:323.

Wesley set forth the ideal of Christian maturity in this way: cleansing from *all* sin and being filled with love to the exclusion of sin. John Wesley saw that this hope of cleansing was possible in this lifetime, and he set it out as the ideal for which all Christians should aim.

The Experience of Christian Perfection

John Wesley's teaching was also informed by people's experience of Christian Perfection, mainly sourced from accounts of the experience of Perfection among the Methodist people.[16] John Wesley never claimed the experience for himself, and even had seasons of doubting the spiritual experiences he did claim.[17] Yet, John Wesley drew from a vast collection of the experiences of others, publishing many of them.[18]

Like Wesley, theologian Leo Cox affirms the importance of taking experience into account when seeking theological definition. In discussing definitions in Wesleyan theology he writes,

---

15. Wesley, Sermon 40, "Christian Perfection", §II. 26-27 in *Works*, 2:119.

16. In his letters Wesley even cited his conversations with those who experienced Perfection as he systematically argued for the doctrine. For example, see John Wesley to Samuel Furly, Dublin, July 30, 1762, in *Letters* 4:186. John Wesley to Miss March, Bristol, October 13, 1765, in *Letters* 4:313.

17. Most scholars point to the lack of any claim of Perfection, and even Wesley's outright denial as evidence he did not have the experience of Perfection. For example, see the letter from John Wesley to the Editor of 'Lloyd's Evening Post', London, March 5, 1767, in *Letters*, 5:43. Furthermore, the Scripture text for the 1741 sermon on Christian Perfection is Philippians 3:12: "Not as though I had already attained, either were already perfect." (Wesley, "Christian Perfection", *Works*, 2:99). It has been suggested by theologian O. A. Curtis that John did experience Perfection, although Curtis' interpretation is unique to him and unjustified in light of the evidence he cited of a spiritual experience recorded in Wesley's journal which is a powerful encounter with God, but not consistent with the Perfection narratives of other Methodists included in this study. O. A. Curtis, *The Christian Faith* (New York: The Methodist Book Concern, 1905), 374-377. In regard to other spiritual experiences, John Wesley expressed his doubts of even his experience of assurance of pardon in a letter to Charles Wesley in 1766. This letter is an interesting artifact as it speaks to the importance Wesley placed on his experience, falling into despair when the winds of emotion changed. Yet, he did assert that with or without the accompanying positive feelings, he was sure of the truth of the message they preached, including both assurance of pardon and Perfection in that message. John Wesley to Charles Wesley, Whithaven, June 27, 1766, in *Letters*, 5:15-16.

18. Thomas Albin did a statistical study of Methodist narratives discovering 245 accounts of Perfection among the published sources and manuscripts he studied. Thomas R Albin, "An Empirical Study of Early Methodist Spirituality," in *Wesleyan theology today: a bicentennial theological consultation*, ed. Theodore Runyon (Nashville : Kingswood Books, 1985), 279.

> Actually no one can understand the love of God until he has felt the inward workings of the Spirit of God. In other words, no one can really understand forgiveness, new life, or sanctification until these are experienced in the soul. For most people what is needed most is not a definition, but an experience, and then a sufficient working definition is found.[19]

Cox expresses how theological ideas are understood in deeper ways through experience. In regards to Christian Perfection, Wesley's teaching shows the importance of both the definition and the experience.

> Furthermore, Wesley asserted the importance of experience for describing Christian Perfection both by using experiential language to describe Perfection and by transmitting the narratives of the Methodist people. For example, in Wesley's letters he casts a vision of Perfection using language that refers to experiences of holiness. Furthermore, as he encouraged new converts to press on toward Perfection, he insisted that even the experience of pressing on functioned to provoke spiritual growth.[20]

Wesley also encouraged those who had experienced Perfection to tell their narrative. For example, in a letter to Mrs. Bennis he encourages her to share her spiritual account: "One reason why those who are saved from sin should freely declare it to believers is because nothing is a stronger incitement to them to seek after the same blessing."[21] Wesley's encouragement to spread Perfection narratives was not only to inspire more people to seek holiness, but also to quiet the detractors who claimed that Perfection was not possible in this life. In addition, Wesley transmitted written narratives of Perfection when he published these stories in his journal, recounting the testimonies of those

---

19. Leo George Cox, *John Wesley's Concept of Perfection* (Kansas City, Missouri: Beacon Hill Press, 1964), 109.

20. For example, see John Wesley to Miss March, Stroud, March 14, 1768, in *Letters*, 5:81-82. John Wesley to Ann Bolton, Londonderry, May 27, 1772, in *Letters*, 5:319. John Wesley to John Mason, London, January 10, 1774, in Letters 6:66. John Wesley to Elizabeth Ritchie, London, January 19, 1782, in *Letters*, 6:102.

21. John Wesley to Mrs. Bennis, Manchester, March 29, 1766, in *Letters*, 5:6.

he met.[22] Moreover, he published further Perfection accounts the *Arminian Magazine*.[23]

In addition to transmitting Perfection narratives, Wesley described the experience of Christian Perfection when he defended that the experience happens in an instant. For example, in a letter to Methodist preacher Joseph Benson, Wesley writes,

> This [is what] I [call] sanctification (which is both an instantaneous and a gradual work), or perfection, the being perfected in love, filled with love, which still admits of a thousand degrees … an entire deliverance from sin, a recovery of the whole image of God, the loving God with all our heart, soul, and strength. And you believe God is able to give you this — yea, to give it you in an instant. You trust He will.[24]

Wesley includes a theological foundation of Perfection as love and the restoration of God's image, which is set alongside receiving the experience by faith.

Furthermore, Wesley notes that the experience of sanctification is both gradual and instantaneous. John Wesley uses the example of death to explain his position. One can be dying for quite some time, but there is only one instant in which one moves from life to death.[25] Likewise, one can be in the process of sanctification for quite some time before the instantaneous experience of Christian Perfection which transforms the believer.

Theologian Albert Outler offers insight into Wesley's understanding of the gradual and instantaneous nature of Christian Perfection. He observes that Wesley focused on the biblical word "perfect" or "perfection" which is the Greek word *teleios*, or goal. Furthermore, Wesley was informed by the Eastern Christian understanding of this concept. Outler notes: "in this view, 'perfection' may be 'realized' in a given moment (always as a gift from God,

---

22. For example, John Wesley, March 6, 1760, *Journal and Diaries IV: 1755-65*, ed. W. Reginald Ward, vol. 21 of *The Bicentennial Edition of The Works of John Wesley*, ed. Frank Baker (Nashville: Abingdon Press, 1992), 243. For more on this example, see chapter 1, pages 36-37.

23. For example, the *Arminian Magazine*, volume 4 (1781) includes a significant number of perfection narratives with Christian Perfection as the focus of the majority of the letters and life accounts.

24. John Wesley to Joseph Benson, London, Dec 28, 1770, in *Letters* 5:215. Another description of Perfection is: "deep communion with the Father and the Son, whereby they are enabled to give Him their whole heart, to love every man as their own soul, and to walk as Christ also walked." John Wesley to Lawrence Coughlan, August 27, 1768, in *Letters* 5:103.

25. Wesley, *Plain Account of Christian Perfection*, 6th ed., §19. 47.

received by trusting faith), yet never as a finished state."[26] In light of this, Outler suggests that the idea of *'perfecting'* is more accurate than 'perfect' in representing Wesley's thinking.[27]

Although Wesley affirmed the importance of the Perfection experience, not all claims to Christian Perfection were received by Wesley as genuine. There was a group that taught that Perfection was necessary for salvation. This teaching was rejected in the Methodist movement for Wesley asserted that salvation is a grace and can exist without the further grace of sanctification.[28] The Perfectionist controversy (described in chapter one) includes other examples of those who claimed the experience in ways that do not align with the teaching of the Wesleys.

Therefore, when Wesley encountered professors of the experience of Perfection, he did not depend solely on testimony of the instantaneous experience of Perfection; rather the proof of those professing Perfection was found in the fruit of the experience.[29] The resulting transformation of character was testimony to the genuineness of the spiritual encounter. In a letter to Miss March, Wesley describes a group of people in Bristol who had experienced Perfection and were transformed:

> There are now about twenty persons here who believe they are saved from sin (1) because they always love, pray, rejoice, and give thanks; and (2) because they have the witness of it in themselves.[30]

The fruit of transformation is described using virtues listed in 1 Thessalonians 5:16-18;[31] each are observable characteristics in the life of the believer.

---

26. Albert C. Outler, "John Wesley: Folk-theologian," *Theology Today* 34, no. 2 (July 1, 1977): 158.

27. While Outler's suggestion to understand sanctification as "perfecting" rather than "perfect" is intriguing, in this book the terminology of "Christian Perfection" will be retained for clarity of understanding while the idea of continued growth and perfecting will be illustrated in the narratives of the Methodist people.

28. Wesley provides encouragement to Elizabeth Hardy who was affected by this teaching. John Wesley to Elizabeth Hardy, Dublin, April 5, 1758, in *Letters* 4:10-13. See also Rack, *Reasonable Enthusiast*, 335.

29. "Q: What is reasonable proof? How may we certainly know one that is saved from all in? ... if it appeared that all his subsequent words and actions were holy and unblamable." Wesley, *Plain Account of Christian Perfection*, §19, 42.

30. Wesley to Miss March, in *Letters*, 4:313.

31. "Now we exhort you, brethren, warn them that are unruly, comfort the feebleminded, support the weak, be patient toward all men. See that none render evil for evil unto any man; but ever follow that which is good, both among yourselves, and to all men. Rejoice evermore. Pray without ceasing. In every

As the Perfectionist controversy in London intensified, Wesley published a short tract directed to those claiming the experience of Perfection called *Cautions and Directions Given to the Greatest Professors in the Methodist Societies*.[32] The tract cautioned those who claimed the experience of Perfection against pride, antinomianism, and schism. He writes,

> You need give it no general name, neither "perfection," "sanctification," "the second blessings," nor "the having attained." Rather speak of the particulars which God has wrought. You may say, "I then felt an unspeakable change. And since that time, I have not felt pride or anger or unbelief, nor any thing but a fulness of love to God and to all mankind."[33]

Wesley advised them to focus on their experience of transformation rather than on labels, and he encouraged them to share their narrative with others.

John Wesley provides a significant amount of teaching on Christian Perfection, but the abundance of teaching on the subject should not be confused with consensus among Methodists. This brief survey now turns to Charles Wesley as one example of the diversity of teaching on Perfection among the early Methodists.

Charles Wesley's teaching on Christian Perfection

The theological position held by Charles Wesley has often been assumed to coincide with that of his older brother John, but recent scholarship has asserted that they indeed held variant positions on some issues, Christian Perfection among them.[34] A summary of Charles' position is presented here through the

---

thing give thanks: for this is the will of God in Christ Jesus concerning you." 1 Thessalonians 5:14-18 (KJV)

32. "Cautions" was published only once in 1762; later it was incorporated into *Farther Thoughts on Christian Perfection*. Yet, as a stand alone tract at the historical moment of the Perfectionist controversy, it offers insight into the boundaries of the experience of Christian Perfection. The tract can be found in John Wesley, "Cautions and Directions Given to the Greatest Professors in the Methodist Societies," in *John Wesley: a Representative Collection of his Writings*, ed. Albert Outler (New York : Oxford University Press, 1964), 298–305. See also Gunter, *Love Divine*, 212.

33. Wesley, "Cautions and Directions," 304.

34. Gareth Lloyd, "'A Cloud of Perfect Witnesses': John Wesley and the London Disturbances 1760-1763," *The Asbury Theological Journal*, vol. 56 no. 2 - vol. 57, no 1 (2001-2002): 118. John Wesley to Charles Wesley, September 1762, in *Letters*, 4:187. For a discussion on the problem of discerning Charles' and John's influence on the published sources, see John R. Tyson, *Charles Wesley on*

work of scholar John Tyson, who has constructed Charles Wesley's theology in regards to sanctification, using sources such as the few surviving manuscripts of original sermons and his large corpus of hymns.[35]

Charles was formed in his doctrine of sanctification similarly to John. They both had been seeking holiness for years before the revival broke out. One example of the aspiration for holiness in Charles' life is that during his time at Oxford he was mentored by William Law who taught on holiness. Tyson notes, "Under William Law's tutelage the Wesleys caught a vision of Christian Perfection and a desire for purity of heart that remained with them for the rest of their lives."[36] The limitation of the vision of Perfection held by Charles in his early years is seen in hindsight after his experience of assurance of forgiveness on Pentecost Sunday in 1738. He writes in his journal on August 10, 1739, relating a conversation with William Law: "I told him, he was my schoolmaster to bring me to Christ; but the reason I did not come sooner to [Christ], was, my seeking to be sanctified before I was justified."[37] Wesley's thoughts on holiness reflects how sanctification fits into a wider context of salvation that also includes assurance of faith or justification. Moreover, it is clear that Charles Wesley's thoughts on Perfection were shaped by his early learning and amended by his experience of justification.

Wesley continued to proclaim holiness as the aim of the Christian life throughout the revival and the emergence of the Methodist communities. The main evidence of his affirmation of holiness is in his hymns. Wesley's hymns were collected for the use of the Methodist communities, attested to by the multitude of quotations of his hymns found in the narratives of the Methodist people. Thus, the theology found in the hymns is an important source for understanding Perfection in the Methodist communities.

Tyson observes three things about Wesley's doctrine of sanctification. First, justification and sanctification are intrinsically linked. The hope coming from justification, as sung in the hymns, leads on immediately to seeking sanctification. Wesley's hymnic offering of hope for holiness flows out of an experience of justification. Whereas John Wesley's defence of doctrines

---

Sanctification: A Biographical and Theological Study (Grand Rapids: Francis Asbury Press, 1986), 47-50, 259-261.

35. Tyson, *Charles Wesley on Sanctification*. See pages 48-50 for a discussion on sources.

36. Tyson, *Assist Me to Proclaim: The Life and Hymns of Charles Wesley* (Grand Rapids: Eerdmans, 2007), 16.

37. Tyson, *Charles Wesley*, 32. Tyson, *Assist*, 16. Charles Wesley, *The Journal of The Rev. Charles Wesley, M.A.* ed. Thomas Jackson (Grand Rapids: Baker, 1980), 1:159.

created distinctions, Charles Wesley's hymns have the singer flowing through justification and sanctification as one soteriological movement.[38]

Second, for Charles, Perfection and holiness are not about moral achievement, but rather inner renewal, even to the extent of restoring the image of God in sinful humanity which has been distorted by the fall.[39] Therefore, Tyson observes, "Charles Wesley's soteriological optimism in propounding a theology of 'full salvation' or Christian perfection was an optimism not about human nature per se but about God's grace and redemptive power."[40] While John was in debates about what the perfected Christian could or could not do (an argument about sin), the Perfection suggested by Charles' hymns points toward restoration rather than sinlessness.

Third, the hymns of Charles Wesley are aspirational. They long for Perfection, emphasizing the quest for holiness over the attainment.[41] Charles offered the hope of Perfection received at the deathbed, and he offered evidence of it in faithful death narratives recorded in his journal. In this hope it is seen how Christian Perfection is the goal of the Christian life. This hope of moving toward Perfection throughout life is fitting for the genre of hymns sung corporately. This is because Wesley's hymns allow the singer to enter into the narrative offered in the hymn, and because continuing to aspire after holiness is the work of all Christians.

In contrast, the narrative of attainment would be unsuited to corporate hymns since not all Methodists had an experience of Christian Perfection.[42]

Like Wesley, historian David Hempton draws attention to holiness as the goal of the Christian life. Hempton offers a metaphor for seeing Methodism

> as a moving vortex, fuelled by scripture and divine love, shaped by experience, reason, and tradition, and moving dynamically towards holiness or Christian perfection. Any model [for Methodism] that lacks dynamic movement toward holiness and its growth within individuals and its dissemination throughout the world is clearly inadequate.[43]

---

38. Tyson, *Charles Wesley*, 42.
39. Ibid., 166, 168.
40. Ibid., 55.
41. Tyson, *Charles Wesley*, 236.
42. Tyson comments on Wesley's style of hymn writing that allows the singer to enter into the biblical stories, rather than just recount them. Tyson, *Charles Wesley*, 25.
43. Hempton, *Empire of the Spirit*, 57.

Indeed, Charles Wesley's aspirational hymns that long for Perfection are examples of the vortex of Methodism moving toward holiness.

Thus, Charles boldly disagreed with his brother John about the doctrine of Christian Perfection. The primary question about Perfection which the brothers disagreed on was *when* in life to expect Perfection. In a letter from John to Charles, it is clear that both brothers affirm that Perfection is possible before death. John questioned Charles for his opinion on when Perfection could happen. John writes,

> As to the time. I believe this instant [when Perfection occurs] generally is the instant of death, the moment before the soul leaves the body. But I believe it may be ten, twenty, or forty years before death. Do we agree or differ here?[44]

John offers logic to support his position, that if God can work Perfection at the point of death, then he can work that grace at any time.[45] Charles was more skeptical and hesitant to declare Perfection in this life too soon.[46]

Another way that Charles differed from John was his tendency to be more critical of the claims of Perfection from the Methodist people. Charles was generally more skeptical of the enthusiastic events of the early revival.[47] While John was judged to be easily taken in by people, Charles was more aware of the effects of emotion on the narratives professed and he would probe for more information.[48] In a letter John notes Charles' unbelief of those who claimed the experience, and Charles even wrote hymns directed at those who claimed the experience to warn them against complacency.[49] Yet, Charles should not be

---

44. John Wesley to Charles Wesley, London, January 27, 1767, in *Letters*, 5:39. Interestingly, if Charles answered, he held little sway with his brother because the most of the content of this letter was later published in the *Arminian Magazine* as statements, rather than questions. *Arminian Magazine*, 6(1783)156-157. This same letter also appears as a duplicate in *Letters*, 4:187 dated September 1762, the 1767 date correlates with the date cited in the *Arminian Magazine* publication. In addition, an ongoing correspondence about their differences on Perfection occurs in 1766–1767, making the later date more likely to be accurate. See also Tyson, *Charles Wesley*, 246–247, 259–261.

45. John Wesley, Sermon 43, "The Scripture Way of Salvation," §III.18 in *Sermons II*, 2:169.

46. Tyson, *Charles Wesley*, 247.

47. Tyson, *Assist*, 60. Also note: "The short remains of my life are devoted to this very thing, to follow your sons [the preachers] ... with buckets of water, and quench the flame of strife and division which they have, or may kindle" Charles Wesley to John Wesley, Oct 23, 1756 in Frank Baker, *Charles Wesley: As Revealed by His Letters*, revised ed. (Madison, NJ: The Charles Wesley Society, 1995), 97.

48. Tyson, *Charles Wesley*, 19. See also John Wesley to Charles Wesley, London, February 12, 1767, in *Letters*, 5:41.

seen simply as a skeptic of testimony. His concern was that those who reached Perfection must be aware of the risk of spiritual pride in "having attained," which would then hinder further growth in grace after the experience.[50]

A number of aspects of Christian Perfection are seen in the teaching of John and Charles Wesley. First, John Wesley defined Perfection from biblical sources. Wesley reiterated the biblical command to be perfect, as our Heavenly Father is perfect; as well, the biblical vision of holiness included not only Perfection but also purity, love and restoration. Second, John Wesley delineates that Christian Perfection is not sinless perfection. The Perfection of early Methodism allows for mistakes, and calls for continued growth in grace. Third, Perfection is both gradual and instantaneous. Furthermore, the evidence of that growth over time in a believer is not the presence of an instantaneous experience; rather, the fruit of holiness is the test for the one who experienced Perfection. Finally, Christian Perfection is the goal of the Christian life seen in Charles Wesley's emphasis on aspiring for Christian Perfection, something for which all believers continue to long.

The summary above of the teaching of John and Charles Wesley on the topic of Christian Perfection also provides definition of the term Christian Perfection. Yet, this attempt to define the term raises the question of how the Methodist people themselves described Christian Perfection. Therefore, the following chapter is a survey of the language used in relation to the experience of Christian Perfection as found in a sample of Methodist Perfection narratives.

---

49. John Wesley to Charles Wesley, Stockton, July 9, 1766, in *Letters*, 5:19-21. Also see John Wesley to Charles Wesley, London, February 12, 1767, in *Letters* 5:40-41. Tyson, *Charles Wesley*, 254, 271.

50. Tyson, *Charles Wesley*, 254.

3

The Language of Perfection Narratives

It is no wonder you should many times be at a loss how to express what you feel. The language of men is too weak to describe the deep things of God.

— John Wesley to Ann Bolton, 1773[1]

It was then that Jesus appeared more glorious than the sun at noonday: giving me power to believe and to receive him for my All, with such a weight of love as pen cannot describe. He spoke into my heart, *Be thou holy:* and *I have sprinkled thee with clean water* and *thou shalt be clean.* The scripture I was before delivered by, was now again sealed upon my heart: and he united me to himself with those words, *I will never leave thee, nor forsake thee.* I found his Spirit bearing witness in the clearest manner, that the work was done.

— Mrs. E. M—n to John Wesley, 1762[2]

The second epigraph above, from a letter to John Wesley, is just one example of the flood of language that crowds into an account of the experience of Christian Perfection. The Methodist people themselves, in addition to the leaders of the movement, can illuminate the doctrine of Perfection as understood in the eighteenth century through the language they used to describe their experiences.

In reading numerous accounts of Christian Perfection it becomes apparent that there is no consistent term used in regards to this experience in the early Methodist communities. The term "Christian Perfection" is rare in the narratives themselves, yet, no other singular term is significantly used for these similar experiences. The early Methodist people did not use the same words

---

1. John Wesley to Ann Bolton, May 2, 1773, in *Letters*, 6:25.
2. Mrs. E. M—n to John Wesley, Potto, March 11, 1762, in *Arminian Magazine*, 4 (1781) 395.

to describe either the process of sanctification, or the instantaneous event that some experienced. I looked for patterns because a unified linguistic pattern might have pointed to dominant teaching coming down from leaders such as John and Charles Wesley, or a consolidated theological idea that had already formed in Methodist circles. Instead, I found that the diversity of terms suggests a multiplicity of theological ideas of Christian Perfection marked the movement, and that Methodists themselves were still searching for words to describe this experience. The diversity notwithstanding, the narratives often reflect the assumption that the reader is familiar with the theological idea behind the experience; rarely is the Perfection experience explained theologically to the reader.

Instead of a single term, the language found in the narratives is descriptive rather than theological, clustered around four themes: love, salvation, God's presence, and transformation. These themes account for most of the references to Perfection. In a few cases the term "Perfection" itself is used, although these cases usually refer to the doctrine rather than the experience of the individual.[3]

Before surveying the narratives, it is worth noting that John Wesley is equally diverse as the Methodist people in his use of language regarding Perfection. He uses the term "Perfection" more often than the narratives do, which reflect that he speaks more often about the doctrine itself. However, all four of the above mentioned themes can be found in Wesley's journal, sermons and letters. Language of love, salvation, God's presence and transformation are all used in contexts clearly equated with Perfection and sanctification.[4] As noted in chapter two, John Wesley did not claim to have experienced Perfection; therefore, his vocabulary as he described his own experience cannot be set alongside these narratives. Nevertheless, the language seen in the narratives of the people is also used by John Wesley as he describes the experiences of others and exhorts the people to seek holiness. Additionally, examining Wesley's

---

3. For examples of occurrences of the doctrine referred to as "Perfection" or "Christian Perfection," see Hunter to Wesley, in *Early Methodist Preachers*, 2:248. Crosby, *Holy Women*, 29 (there is a problem with the pagination in *Holy Women*; this citation is for the second page 29). Clark, *Arminian Magazine*, 6:302. Matthias Joyce, "The Life of Mr. Matthias Joyce", in *The Lives of Early Methodist Preachers Chiefly Written by Themselves*, ed. Thomas Jackson, 3rd ed., 6 vols. (London: Wesleyan Conference Office, 1878), 4:270.

4. For examples of these various images, see Wesley, Sermon 43, "Scripture Way of Salvation", §§III.12-14, 2:167. "Constant communion with God the Father and Son fills their hearts with humble love. Now this is what I always did and do now mean by 'perfection'," Wesley, March 6, 1760, *Journal V*, in *Works*, 21:245. See also Wesley, Dec 29, 1766, *Journal V*, in *Works*, 22:68. Wesley, June 2, 1768, *Journal V*, in *Works*, 22:147. For a brief discussion on Wesley's diversity of terms, see Harald Lindström, *Wesley and Sanctification*, 127. For a discussion of Charles Wesley's use of salvation language surrounding sanctification, see Tyson, *Charles Wesley*, 56.

writing in search of the variety of terms used in the narratives reveals that John Wesley referred to Christian Perfection using the same diversity of language as the Methodist people. This larger lexicon of Perfection increases the references to both the doctrine and of experience of Perfection found in Wesley's works. By observing the terms used by the Methodist people also found in Wesley's works, it is clear that the language used by Wesley is consistent with the narratives in both variety of the terms and themes.

Love is the first theme we will examine. Love appears in each of the four central narratives examined in this book, as well as in many other Perfection narratives. When describing the affective experience of Christian Perfection, the language of love is most often used. These narratives are the story of an individual's experience, rarely a philosophical or theological explanation for that experience. These experiences are marked by a palpable sensation interpreted by the subject to be love.

The love described in the narratives is God's love experienced in people's own hearts. This love is described using superlatives such as perfect, pure, full or holy.[5] Moreover, this love is active: it showers down, fills an ocean, redeems, perfects, sanctifies, fills the heart and is like fire.[6] Sarah Crosby evokes a rich image as she describes her encounter with God saying that her "soul seemed all love," as if any sin or fear was crowded out by God's love.[7]

The love experienced and expressed in these Perfection narratives was from God and was effortlessly imparted to the believer. There was no work on the part of the subject to earn the love bestowed. Furthermore, love transformed the person whom it filled and multiplied itself as it caused the believer to show love to others, which can be particularly seen in the narrative of Bathsheba Hall in chapter nine.[8] The lexicon of love used in the narratives illuminates Christian Perfection because an experience primarily based in love challenges any sense

---

5. Hall, *Arminian Magazine*, 4:96, 197. Clark, *Arminian Magazine*, 6:20, 21, 22, 188, 245, 300. Crosby, *Holy Women*, 29 (second 29), 65. Thomas Walsh, "The Life and Death of Mr. Thomas Walsh," in *The Lives of Early Methodist Preachers Chiefly Written by Themselves*, ed. Thomas Jackson, 3rd ed., 6 vols. (London: Wesleyan Conference Office, 1878), 3:220. Mary Fletcher, *The Life of Mrs. Mary Fletcher*, ed. Henry Moore (New York: Soule & Mason,1818), 45. Hester Ann Rogers, *An Account of the Experience of Mrs. H. A. Rogers* (London: T. Cordeux, 1818), 44.

6. Hall, *Arminian Magazine*, 4:195, 310. Clark, *Arminian Magazine*, 6:245. Hunter to Wesley in *Early Methodist Preachers*, 2:248, 250. Joyce, "Life," in *Early Methodist Preachers*, 4:271.

7. Crosby, *Holy Women*, 2:33. In this section of Crosby's account, the hymn lines "Christ was all in all to me; and all my heart was love" is quoted in two Perfection narratives, sounding the same image of love overwhelming. An unnamed writer to John Wesley, June 4, 1761, in *Arminian Magazine*, 4:164. Rogers, *Account*, 47.

8. See chapter nine, pages 104-105.

of striving or selfish perfectionism which might be found in the concept of Christian Perfection.

In addition to love, salvation language is used in reference to Christian Perfection. The early Methodists were seeking salvation that is full, complete, inward — a greater salvation, even "the Great Salvation."[9] These references in the Perfection narratives about salvation are not references to conversion, or justification because the longing for salvation is coming from those who had already experienced a significant conversion experience.

The language of salvation is often paired with reference to sin. The salvation is both greater and inward because it saves the believer from sin experienced after conversion.[10] The anxiety created when sin is discovered after conversion requires a deeper or fuller salvation. Yet, it must be noted that conversion or justification was indeed enough to assure the believer of their eternal salvation, Christian Perfection was desired, but not necessary for the Christian life.[11]

Third, there is language attributing the experience of Christian Perfection to God's presence. God's presence signals the divine source of the encounter, and His abiding presence is part of the result of the divine experience. For example, Ann Gilbert is "filled with the divine presence", George Clark's "soul partakes of the divine nature" and William Hunter's soul is united with Christ.[12] Each narrative uses language that intensifies the subjects experience of God's presence, an experience more significant than their previous experience of God. Furthermore, the presence of God evokes transformation in believers: Clark longs to be holy as God is holy, Sarah Crosby describes a season of pure love as the ability "to walk in the light of his countenance" and Bathsheba Hall tells of a friend who was transformed so that "self is gone; and God is all in

---

9. Hall, *Arminian Magazine*, 4:36, 96, 311. Miss M. B. to John Wesley, February 1761, in *Arminian Magazine*, 4 (1781) 51. Letter from an unnamed man to John Wesley, June 4, 1761, in *Arminian Magazine*, 4 (1781) 164. Clark, *Arminian Magazine*, 6:299. Hunter to Wesley, *Early Methodist Preachers* 2:246, 248. Thomas Rankin, "The Life of Mr. Thomas Rankin," in *The Lives of Early Methodist Preachers Chiefly Written by Themselves*, ed. Thomas Jackson, 3rd ed., 6 vols. (London: Wesleyan Conference Office, 1878), 5:169. Crosby, *Holy Women*, 2:59. Fletcher, *The Life of Mrs. Mary Fletcher*, 44.

10. Hall, *Arminian Magazine*, 4:310. Clark, *Arminian Magazine*, 6:300. Hunter to Wesley, *Early Methodist Preachers*, 2:246, 249.

11. See chapter two (page 22, note 28) for John Wesley's assurance of the sufficiency of justification.

12. Ann Gilbert, "The Experience of Mrs. Ann Gilbert, of Gwinear in Cornwall," in *Arminian Magazine*, 18(1795) 44. Clark, *Arminian Magazine*, 6:407. Compare also where Bathsheba Hall's suggestion of partaking in the divine nature is remedy for the pollutions of the world: Hall, *Arminian Magazine*, 4:150. Hunter to Wesley, *Early Methodist Preachers*, 2:249.

all."[13] The positive and lasting change is evoked by God's presence in a new way.

The witness to the divine presence reinforces that the source of Christian Perfection is from God, not earned or achieved by human effort. In addition, God's presence is both the means and motivation for believers to live a holy life. The presence of unitive language when describing Perfection shifts the doctrine away from moral obedience attempting to earn the favour of God, and proclaims instead the enjoyment of God's presence.

Lastly, when referring to their experience of Christian Perfection, the early Methodists describe the transformation that took place. The language used is quite poetic, evoking the emotions of the transformation even more than communicating theological principles. The most common transformation image is that of cleansing from sin. For the unnamed man's whose story was told through his letter to John Wesley printed in the *Arminian Magazine*, the desire for transformation was expressed as a longing to be cleansed from "all sin."[14] For Bathsheba Hall her longing was for complete deliverance from sin. In her perfection account, her assurance comes through the scripture words: "Thou art all fair, there is no spot in thee" (Song of Songs 4:7)[15] The longing for deliverance from sin led to the transformative experience of being cleansed from inward sin.[16]

The transformation images also include changes that bring about restoration: Bathsheba Hall notes, "The Lord lifted up my head," and William Hunter received "new vigour to [his] spirit."[17] In all of these phrases the language of the Perfection experience is active — change is actively taking place — which shows the transformative power of these experiences for the early Methodists. More about the transformative power of these experiences will be explored in chapter seven through the story of George Clark.

The variety of language used for Perfection offers insight into the nuances of the idea, while at the same time causes the dilemma of how to use language when speaking of these experiences. The term "Christian Perfection" is not sufficient to communicate the nuances of love, full salvation, divine union and transformation that are expressed in the linguistic variety of the narratives. In

---

13. Clark, *Arminian Magazine*, 6:20. Crosby, *Holy Women*, 2:33. Hall, *Arminian Magazine*, 4:196.

14. Unnamed Man to Wesley, *Arminian Magazine*, 4:162.

15. Hall, *Arminian Magazine*, 4:38.

16. For more examples of cleansing from sin see also Thomas Rankin to John Wesley, Rye, March 8, 1762, in *Arminian Magazine*, 4:218; Rankin, "Life," in *Early Methodist Preachers*, 5:169. Fletcher, *The Life of Mrs. Mary Fletcher*, 45.

17. Hall, *Arminian Magazine*, 4:37. Hunter to Wesley, *Early Methodist Preachers*, 2:248.

addition, the term *perfection* can erroneously communicate a moral infallibility or completeness which is inconsistent with what was being experienced. Nevertheless, in this book the term "Christian Perfection" will be used, particularly in reference to the doctrine itself. In reference to the narratives, the language that appears in that narrative will also be used to communicate the diversity of metaphors expressed by the early Methodist people.

4

Narrative as a Sources for Theology

> You need give it no general name, neither "perfection," "sanctification," "the second blessings," nor "the having attained." Rather speak of the particulars which God has wrought. You may say, "I then felt an unspeakable change. And since that time, I have not felt pride or anger or unbelief, nor any thing but a fulness of love to God and to all mankind."
>
> —John Wesley, *Cautions and Directions*, 1762[1]

In a study of Christian Perfection it is easy to seek out what John Wesley thought about the doctrine from his treatise on Perfection or from his sermon on the topic. Less obvious is that there is much to be learned about the theology of Perfection among the early Methodist by listening to their individual stories. In the chapters that follow I will argue for particular theological interpretations of Christian Perfection based on the evidence in the lives of the early Methodists and the narratives told of those lives. To create a foundation for these arguments, I will take a short excursus to discuss the field of narrative theology which emerged as a distinct theological conversation during the twentieth century.

As mentioned in the introduction, I did not start this investigation of Christian Perfection with the narratives of early Methodists, but as my research unfolded the narratives have become the focal point of my study and have led to this book. Narrative is the topic, vehicle and medium of this book. Narrative is not the only source for theology, but for investigating the story of Christian Perfection in the eighteenth century, narrative is a well suited method.

An early research question for this project was to seek out the reception history of John Wesley's teaching on Perfection. Namely, how did the early

---

1. John Wesley, "Cautions and Directions Given to the Greatest Professors in he Methodist Societies," in *John Wesley*, ed. Albert Outler (New York: Oxford University Press, 1964), 304.

Methodists express the doctrine of Christian Perfection that Wesley was teaching. The reception history, as documented through letters and published journals, provides a historical artifact to fill out the picture of this time period; giving context to the theology offered by Wesley. In addition to the value of these narratives as reception history, they go a step further and become the source for understanding the theology of Christian Perfection, because the ideas discussed by Wesley are lived out in the narratives.

Despite the appropriateness of using story as a source of history, the use of narrative in this book raises the question: is narrative a valid source for theological inquiry? I do not claim to offer here a comprehensive summary of the arguments in favour of using narratives to reconstruct theology, but rather I will offer a taste of the academic discussion in order to give a frame to the narratives themselves which will follow in later chapters. I am indebted to the insights of others who have summarized the central points in the development of narrative theology. I will draw on only a few key ideas which are discussed in much more detail elsewhere.[2]

The subject of narrative theology as a significant academic conversation is recent, more recent than Wesley's lifetime. However, this ongoing conversation about understanding theology through narrative provides language to discuss how the early Methodists were appropriating and developing their theology centuries previous.

I will appeal to two ideas to lay the foundation that narrative is not only valid, but the ideal medium for seeking out understanding of the doctrine of Christian Perfection. First, the Christian faith and revelation — specifically the Bible which is the historic and literary source for the Christian faith — is itself narrative in nature. Richard Niebuhr develops this idea in his book *The Meaning of Revelation*.[3] The second reason that narrative is a valid source for theological reflection is that human experience is narrative. That is to say that the experiences of life are linear and then expressed to others through narrative. For this insight I am indebted to Stephen Crites in his essay "The Narrative Quality of Experience."[4]

---

2. For more on the conversation on narrative theology see Gregory Loving, "Narrative and Power Toward a Theology of the Overdog," (PhD. diss., Graduate Theological Union, 2000) 3-55. See also Erica L. Vinskie, "Becoming Catholic: Story, Sacrament, Conversion and the Emergence of Faith in Postconciliar Autobiographies," (M.A. Thesis, Temple University, 2011) 22-26.

3. H. Richard Niebuhr, *The Meaning of Revelation* (New York: MacMillian, 1941).

4. Stephen Crites, "The Narrative Quality of Experience" *Journal of the American Academy of Religion* 39, no. 3 (Sep 1971): 291-311.

Richard Niebuhr contributes to the discussion of narrative theology by positing that the revelation of God comes through history. Further, that the Bible is overwhelmingly narrative in expression and, following the example of scripture, throughout church history narrative has been central to the expression and transmission of the Christian faith. He writes, "the sermons of Peter and Stephen as reported or reconstructed in the book of Acts were recitals of the great events in Christian and Israelite history."[5] And he goes on to note how this continued through church history, in that "the only creed which has been able to maintain itself in the church with any approach to universality consists for the most part of statements about events."[6] These arguments from Niebuhr provide a foundational understanding that the Christian faith is transmitted through story and unfolds through the events of history, therefore theological reflection can be found in narrative.

Niebuhr goes on to explain how history can be either internal history or external history. Internal history being the story of a people and events known by those who are on the inside of the events. External history is therefore observations from outside the experience. Revelation, therefore is primarily internal history.[7] This understanding of the revelation of God to Christian people also helps to build an understanding of how the study of Perfection narratives functions in relation to understanding the doctrine of Perfection. The narratives in this study are very much insight into the doctrine of Perfection from within. Those who interpret their experiences as Christian Perfection are believers that this experience is the way that God has interacted with their soul to bring about their spiritual growth and sanctification.

Further to Niebuhr's insights, Stephen Crites contributes to the conversation about narrative theology in his article "The Narrative Quality of Experience." He offers the argument that "the formal quality of experience through time is inherently narrative."[8]

In explaining his position he offers the insight that life is given meaning through sacred stories, which are larger than one person. Sacred stories are not the stories of daily life created by daily choices, rather one awakens into sacred stories which are the interpretive framework of a culture.[9] While sacred stories are often unspoken, the experiences of life expressed through stories Crites calls mundane stories.[10]

---

5. Niebuhr, *Revelation*, 33.
6. Ibid., 34.
7. Ibid., 44-45.
8. Crites, "Experience," 291.
9. Ibid., 295.

In addition to these reality of the stories present in our lives, he adds a third aspect: "the narrative quality of experience has three dimensions, the sacred story, the mundane story, and the temporal form of experience itself: three narrative tracks, each constantly reflecting and affecting the course of the other."[11] What Crites names as the temporal form of experience is that the drama of the past, present and anticipated future unfold in reality through a linear movement through time. This assertion that narrative is an inherent element of experience supports the inquiry into the spiritual experiences of the early Methodist people as a valid source for building theology. If experience is narrative and temporal, then the theology which gives meaning to experiences can be found in narrative.

Further, Crites describes tension between the memory of the past, the experienced present and the anticipated future which creates the space where drama unfolds and makes it possible for a change in the direction of the story. Even changes to the extent that the unspoken meaning ascribed to experiences through sacred stories is changed. As we will see in the following chapters, the narratives of Christian Perfection of the early Methodists are a prime example of these moments of significant change — a turn in the story.

To use the language of Crites, narratives of Perfection are a linear experience that have a before and an after. Similarly, Neibuhr discusses the centrality of a significant turn in the story in relation to the revelation of God. He argues that the nature of internal history demands that one make a clear choice to enter into that history. He writes, "there is no continuous movement from an objective inquiry into the life of Jesus to a knowledge of him as the Christ who is our Lord. Only a decision of the self, a leap of faith, a *metanoia* or revolution of the mind can lead from observation to participation and from observed to lived history."[12] Niebuhr is saying here, that there is an element of the revelation of God which can only be known from the inside. Similarly, I would argue that the experiences described by early Methodists as Christian Perfection are best understood from the inside, therefore narratives of those who professed to have had experiences of Perfection are key to our understanding of the doctrine.

There is much more that the conversation about narrative theology could offer the narratives in this book, but these few points are sufficient. Narratives are a valid source for inquiry because story is the medium through which the Christian faith is expressed, both in the biblical record and in the creeds of the

10. Ibid., 296.
11. Ibid., 305.
12. Niebuhr, Revelation, 61.

early church. Furthermore, the revelation of God to human beings is relational as God encounters humans in their own internal histories. This is only fitting, as all of human experience is linear and narrative.

5

The Power of Perfection Narratives

Dear Sir,
On May 3, 1757, [a man] was speaking of two persons that were made perfect in love. While he spoke, God said to my heart, 'This is what thou wantest: without it thou canst not be happy.' From that day my convictions were exceeding great… But I believed, 'He has done this for many. He *may* do it for *me*.'

Mrs. E. M—n to John Wesley, 1762[1]

So begins a series of letters to John Wesley from a woman, referred to in publication as "Mrs. E. M—n." These letters were written about her pursuit of Christian Perfection and were published in the *Arminian Magazine* in 1781. This letter provides the historical detail that Mrs. E. M—n's faith narrative was shaped by hearing about how others were made perfect in love, provoking her to seek after God more intensely. It is just one example of how the doctrine of Christian Perfection, while it was defined and taught by key leaders such as John and Charles Wesley, was significantly spread among the early Methodist communities by narratives that embodied the doctrine. These narratives bore witness to an experience of God's love, as well as holiness of life, thus inspiring believers to seek out their own experience of Christian Perfection.

The theological idea of Christian Perfection in the eighteenth century was defended as essential by Wesleyan Methodists.[2] Nuances of the doctrine have been discussed by scholars for centuries since, some in favour of the doctrine and some trying to dismiss elements of the doctrine.[3] Despite the

---

1. Mrs. E. M—n to John Wesley, Potto, March 11, 1762, in *Arminian Magazine*, 4 (1781) 393.

2. In 1790, one year before his death, Wesley expressed the importance of Perfection. He declared: "[the doctrine of Perfection] is the grand depositum which God has lodged with the people called Methodists; and for the sake of propagating this chiefly He appeared to have raised us up." John Wesley to Robert Carr Brackenbury, Bristol, September 15, 1790, in *Letters*, 8:238.

controversy about Christian Perfection, it remains a historical fact that the vision of Christian maturity marked by holiness and God's love was indeed experienced in the early Methodist communities and was transmitted through narratives. In his biography of Wesley, historian Henry Rack makes a brief observation of the curious historical fact of the doctrine of Perfection among the Wesleyan Methodists:

> It has been suggested that the doctrine [of Perfection] was a quirk due to John Wesley's peculiar High Church history and prejudices, unrepresentative of the Revival, or even of Methodism as a whole. Most converts, it could be argued, had their emotions and expectations centred on the joys of conversion. Certainly perfectionism was largely confined to Methodism and controversial within it. But there is also ample evidence, even allowing for Wesley's anxiety to publicize cases, to show that a large number of Methodists at all levels sought for it and believed they had attained it, at least for a time.[4]

My research explores the historical evidence that the Methodist people were pursuing Perfection as noted by Rack. Teaching on Christian Perfection by the leaders of the movement has been dismissed by some scholars as eccentric or as inconsistent with the life of the people.[5] On the contrary, the witness of these narratives shows that a significant number of people in the Methodist communities were seeking and even experiencing Perfection.

In addition to arguing systematically for the doctrine of Perfection in publications such as the *Plain Account of Christian Perfection,* John Wesley recognized the rhetorical power of narrative.[6] Narratives were built into the

---

3. A few examples of scholars wrestling with the idea of Christian Perfection include: R. Newton Flew, "Methodism," in *The Idea of Perfection in Christian Theology: An Historical Study of the Christian Ideal for the Present Life* (Oxford: Clarendon Press, 1934), 313-341, reprinted 1968. Lindström. *Wesley and Sanctification.* Sangster, *The Path to Perfection: An Examination and Restatement of John Wesley's Doctrine of Christian Perfection.*

4. Rack, *Reasonable Enthusiast,* 428. Consider also, "From the mouth of many witnesses we have now received accumulated proof that the doctrine as Wesley taught it was the doctrine his people held and experienced. It would be doing less than justice to the honesty and coherence of those accounts to suggest that their leader had simply imposed his ideas on their mind. The witnesses are so numerous: the accounts are so different in detail, yet so similar in substance, that it is impossible to dismiss them as personal vagaries or odd coincidences." Sangster, *The Path to Perfection,* 130.

5. An example of the dismissive position is the scholar whom Rack references in the above quote, Michael R. Watts, *The Dissenters* (Oxford: Clarendon Press, 1978), 433.

activities of the Methodist communities. For example, the letter days: John and Charles Wesley would travel around to different communities carrying with them letters of spiritual experience to inspire believers. The formal event for sharing letters was the letter-day service where reading letters replaced preaching.[7] Thomas Albin describes letter days saying,

> The noetic focus of the letter day was the increased awareness of the variety of ways that God was at work in the world. The practice was both simple and profound as the people heard new things and responded in prayer and singing. The affective focus was to increase the members' desire for a deeper relationship with God and their trust in God's providential work throughout the world.[8]

Furthermore, the literary expression of letter days is found in the letters section of the *Arminian Magazine*. Wesley included a selection of letters in each edition, beginning with his own collection of letters of spiritual accounts of people in the Methodist movement.[9]

Another platform for narrative in the Methodist communities was the Love-feast. The purpose of the Methodist Love-feast was to share spiritual experiences with each other.[10] For example, Mrs. E. M—n in a second letter in the *Arminian Magazine*, published a month after the letter mentioned previously, tells how she was plunged into God's love while at a Love-feast where John Wesley was sharing.[11] Interestingly, the testimony of Mrs. E. M—n suggests that this sharing of story during the Love-feast was not simply a celebration of what God had already done, but also prompted new encounters with God.

---

6. For examples of systematic argumentation, see John Wesley to Edmund Gibson, in *Letters*, 2:280. John Wesley to William Dodd, March 12, 1756, in *Letters*, 3:167-172. John Wesley, Sermon 43, "The Scripture Way of Salvation," in *Sermons II: 34-70*, ed. Albert C. Outler, vol. 2 of *The Bicentennial Edition of The Works of John Wesley*, ed. Frank Baker (Nashville: Abingdon Press, 1985), 2:153-169. Wesley, Sermon 40, "Christian Perfection," in *Sermons II, 2:97-124*. Wesley, *The Plain Account of Christian Perfection*. Interestingly, in *The Plain Account of Christian Perfection*, Wesley uses narrative to argue his point by narrating the development of the doctrine and including the Perfection account of Jane Cooper.

7. Albin, "Inwardly Persuaded," 56-57.

8. Ibid., 57.

9. Ibid., 57-58.

10. Ibid., 56.

11. Mrs. E. M—n to John Wesley, in *Arminian Magazine*, 4:444-445. See chapter 2, page 17 for an excerpt from this letter.

In addition to encouraging letter days and Love-feasts where a variety of spiritual experiences were shared, John Wesley wrote of the particular mandate to talk about experiences of Christian Perfection. In a letter to Mrs. Bennis he writes,

> One reason why those who are saved from sin should freely declare it to believers is because nothing is a stronger incitement to them to seek after the same blessing. And we ought by every possible means to press every serious believer to forget the things which are behind and with all earnestness go on to perfection. Indeed, if they are not thirsting after this, it is scarce possible to keep what they have: they can hardly retain any power of faith if they are not panting after holiness.[12]

Wesley urges Mrs. Bennis to share her experience of Perfection because of how central holiness is to the life of the believer, and he communicates his confidence in the power of sharing the narrative of Perfection as an effective tool to evoke holiness. This letter is an example of how Wesley encouraged those who had experienced Perfection to spread their narratives in the community, even though Wesley had not experienced Perfection himself.[13]

Another example of narrative transmission of Christian Perfection was told in the *Arminian Magazine*. This letter tells the story of an unnamed man who sought out a friend who had reportedly received a clean heart, or Perfection. He was skeptical but curious about the claim. He writes, "A little while after, I spoke to her: but it was as if the Lord had put a bridle in my jaws. I could not contradict. I could only say at last, 'If you have this blessing, pray that I may have it also.'"[14] Although doubtful when approaching his friend, he went away seeking freedom from sin more intensely. His letter continues and bears witness to his own experience of Christian Perfection, a release from sin that came while he was praying with friends.[15]

Furthermore, a multi-layered example of the transmission of Perfection is found in John Wesley's published journal. The entry for March 6, 1760 includes a transcribed letter recounting the experience of M— S— of Birmingham. The story begins with the public testimony of "one who thought she had

---

12. Wesley to Bennis, in *Letters*, 5:6.

13. See chapter two, page 21, note 17, for a discussion of John Wesley's lack of an experience of Christian Perfection.

14. An unnamed writer to John Wesley, June 4, 1761, in *Arminian Magazine*, 4:163.

15. Ibid. 4:163-164.

received that blessing" on January 30, 1760 which spurred M— S— on to seek Perfection.[16] The layers of transmission unfold: the public testimony to Christian Perfection impacted the listener, M— S—, who then wrote the account for Wesley, who then published it in his journal for others to read.[17] The chain of narrative passed through the Methodist structures that used public testimony and publishing to spread the narratives of Perfection.

Although narrative serves as a vehicle of transmission of the doctrine of Perfection, the power of narrative is that it also embodies aspects of the doctrine not so easily expressed in propositional rhetoric. The literature that John Wesley produced arguing for the possibility of Christian Perfection is convincing, yet the narratives of lives transformed embody Christian Perfection in unique ways. For example, the struggle with sin before the experience of Perfection is made real in the journals of these ordinary Methodists. Then the transformation has the result of freedom from sin after an experience of cleansing, which is seen in the journal writer as ongoing hopefulness in the journal entries. The freedom from real sin is just one nuance of the experience among many that can be observed when lives are examined, not solely a doctrine disputed. We now turn to the task of listening to the story of Christian Perfection as lived out in the eighteenth century by the early Methodists.

---

16. John Wesley, March 6, 1760, *Journal and Diaries IV: 1755-65*, ed. W. Reginald Ward, vol. 21 of *The Bicentennial Edition of The Works of John Wesley*, ed. Frank Baker (Nashville: Abingdon Press, 1992), 21:243.

17. Interestingly, this volume of the journal was first published in 1765, soon after the Perfectionist controversy occurred in London.

PART II

NARRATIVES OF PERFECTION:
Four Early Methodists

6

Sarah Crosby and Longing for Perfection

> I have enjoyed many reviving seasons for these last few months, blessed by my Lord. But I long for deeper manifestations of the divine nature. O, when shall I be overwhelmed with thy delightful presence.
> — Sarah Crosby, journal entry, June 3rd, 1800[1]

In a letterbook Sarah Crosby (1729-1804) preserved her communications with John Wesley in 1772 and 1773 about Christian Perfection. Wesley asks, "Do you see Christian Perfection now in the same light you did Twenty or Ten Years ago?... And do you experience now what you did then?"[2] Crosby replies,

> in answer to your question, dear Sir, whether I now experience what I did then? I freely acknowledge I have not uninterruptedly enjoyed so great a degree of the glorious liberty wherewith Christ made me free sixteen years past, as I did then... And glory be to his adorable name, I now find him as precious and present with me as ever. He is the center of all my hopes, the end of my enlarged desires.[3]

Wesley responds, "My Dear Sister, You judge right.... I see more & more the Absolute Necessity of always thinking & speaking of Perfection in the most Simple Manner possible... It is nothing more, nothing less, than Pure Love, Humble, Gentle, Patient Love filling the Heart & ruling the Life."[4] Reading

---

1. Sarah Crosby, *Biographical Sketches of the Lives and Public Ministry of Various Holy Women, whose eminent usefulness and successful labours in the Church of Christ, have entitled them to be enrolled among the great benefactors of mankind: In which are included several letters from the Rev. J. Wesley never before published*, ed. Z. Taft (London, 1825), 2:107.

2. John Wesley to Sarah Crosby, London, October 18, 1772, in Frank Baker, "John Wesley and Sarah Crosby," *Proceedings of the Wesley Historical Society* 27 no. 4 (Dec 1949): 80.

3. Sarah Crosby to John Wesley, Cross Hall, Jan 26, 1773, in *Early Methodist Spirituality: Selected Women's Writings*, ed. Paul Wesley Chilcote (Nashville: Kingswood, 2007), 267.

this exchange of ideas about Christian Perfection provokes questions about this woman who boldly engaged with John Wesley on the doctrine of Perfection. I cannot help but want to know more about Sarah Crosby and the experience she had which allowed her to speak to John Wesley with such authority.

Sarah Crosby was an active member of the Methodist community and a close friend of John Wesley. There are historical sources for her life in letters she wrote as well as portions of her journal were preserved through publication after her death.[5] In addition to the published sources, a letterbook is housed in the archives at Duke University. Crosby's life and narrative comes alive in this letterbook where she copied letters which she received and wrote, and she used part of the book as a journal — such everyday occurrences.[6] In addition, there are references to Crosby in letters from other Methodists and in John Wesley's diary.[7] Crosby's story concludes with a letter from her friend, Anne Tripp, giving the account of Crosby's faithful death.[8] These sources, taken together, give a significant picture of the spirituality of Sarah Crosby. In her writing is a lifelong portrait of humble longing for Christian Perfection.

Sarah Crosby's Story

Sarah Crosby was born on November 7, 1729, and historian Frank Baker suggests she was born in the Leeds area of England.[9] In a 1757 letter to John Wesley, Crosby tells of her early spiritual experiences and her conversion. She had been presented with Christianity from a young age, and she hungered for an assurance of forgiveness.[10] Under the preaching of a Mr. Andrews (identified

---

4. John Wesley to Sarah Crosby, London, February 3, 1773, in Baker, "John Wesley and Sarah Crosby," 81. The manuscript letterbook appears to record the date of this letter as February 9, while Baker published this letter as February 3.

5. Sarah Crosby, "The Grace of God Manifested, In an Account of Mrs. Crosby, of Leeds," *Methodist Magazine* 29 (1806): 418-423, 465-473, 517-521, 563-568, 610-617. The *Methodist Magazine* is the continuation of the *Arminian Magazine*. The same memoir was published in Crosby, *Holy Women*, 2:23-114.

6. Frank Baker writes about the letterbook and Crosby in Baker, "John Wesley and Sarah Crosby," 76-82. I had the opportunity to examine the letterbook at Duke University, June 17, 2009.

7. John Wesley, July 22, 1789, *Journal and Diaries VII* (1787-1791), ed. W. Reginald Ward and Richard P. Heitzenrater, vol. 24 of *The Bicentennial Edition of the Works of John Wesley* (Nashville: Abingdon Press, 1997), 521. See also Mary Holder, *Holy Women*, 1:104.

8. Letter from Anne Tripp, in *Holy Women*, 2:112-115. Letter from Anne Tripp, in *Methodist Magazine*, 29 (1806) 615-617.

9. Crosby marks her 70th birthday on Nov 7, 1799, giving us her birthdate. Crosby, *Holy Women*, 2:105. Baker, "John Wesley and Sarah Crosby," 76.

only as a dissenting minister) Crosby received that promised assurance of forgiveness on October 29, 1749, just shy of her twentieth birthday.[11]

After her conversion, Crosby came into contact with the Methodist community. This connection came through the man who would become her husband. Interestingly, history knows Sarah Crosby only by her married name, while little is known about her marriage.[12] Mr. Crosby introduced her to John Wesley's writing, and she eventually sought out Wesley's preaching.[13] About 1750, during the consolidation phase of Methodism, Crosby joined the Methodist society seeking to satisfy her longing for Christian Perfection. The teaching of John and Charles Wesley had evoked within her hope to be transformed; she longed to be filled with love in the way that they described.[14]

As Crosby sought Christian Perfection she was faced with an increasing awareness of her own sinfulness. In her letter to John Wesley she writes,

> The Lord now shewed me more deeply than ever, that I was an unclean thing before him; yet I prayed to know myself as I was known of God, for I could not bear that he should see a link of sin within me, and not know it myself…God continued to give me still deeper knowledge of myself; and most of the evils which I heard of in others, I felt in some degree in my own heart; but pride, selfwill, anger, and unbelief, were most predominant.[15]

Crosby sought more and more knowledge of herself in response to the discovery of sin after her conversion. She writes, "I was now convinced that I had hitherto sought *knowledge*, more than the *love of God*, which error I prayer God to forgive, promising I would now seek his love alone."[16] Crosby shifted from years of focus on sin to seeking God's love, a change that opened her to an

---

10. Sarah Crosby to John Wesley, London, August 17, 1757, in *Holy Women*, 2:28

11. Baker, "John Wesley and Sarah Crosby," 76.

12. The letter written to John Wesley in 1757 recounting her spiritual journey mentions her marriage around 1750, but it does not mention that about six months prior to the letter's composition, her husband had abandoned her. This biographical detail is evident from a comment sixteen years later in her journal. Crosby spent the rest of her life working and living alongside other Methodist women. Baker, "John Wesley and Sarah Crosby," 76-77. Crosby, *Holy Women*, 58.

13. Crosby to Wesley, *Holy Women*, 2:28 (there is a problem with pagination in Holy Women; this citation is for the second page 28).

14. Ibid., 2: 28-29 (second 28-29).

15. Ibid., 2:29 (second 29), 31.

16. Ibid., 2:33. For another narrative of this shift in thinking, see Crosby to Wesley, in *Early Methodist Spirituality*, 265-266.

experience that she would later call "glorious liberty wherewith Christ made me free."[17] Thus, the way was prepared for her experience of Christian Perfection.

From the account found in a selection of letters, it appears that Crosby had an experience (or multiple experiences) which evoked in her a transformation similar to what other Methodists would describe as Christian Perfection.[18] Whereas the journals of other Methodists offer a concise account of their Perfection experience, what follows is Crosby's experience pieced together from various sources.

Crosby's 1757 letter to John Wesley tells how after agonizing about the sin discovered by self-scrutiny, she encountered God:

> At length one day, while I was sitting at work, the Lord Jesus appeared to the eye of my mind surrounded with glory, while his love overwhelmed me; I said, this is the power I have waited for, and was
>
> 'constrained to cry, by love divine,
> My God! thou art for ever mine.'
>
> I now felt my idol was beneath my feet, and so it has remained ever since. My soul seemed all love, and I desired nothing so much, as to lay down my life for others, that they might feel the same.[19]

Crosby expressed how God's presence and the overwhelming love overcame her.

---

17. Crosby to Wesley, in *Early Methodist Spirituality*, 267.

18. The confirmed sources from Sarah Crosby offer less than a clear reference to one particular experience of Christian Perfection. Although there is no certainty that the following comments are from Sarah Crosby, it appears that two letters to John Wesley published as "S. C." in the *Arminian Magazine* confirm the event of Christian Perfection in Sarah Crosby's life. The author of the letters expresses: "O how I long for your full salvation! I can hardly be happy alone." Mrs. S. C. to John Wesley, April 25, 1758, in *Arminian Magazine* 4 (1781) 668. In an additional letter: "Your propositions concerning Christian Perfection, are exactly agreeable to the sentiments of my heart. Ever since God has wrought this work in me, I have daily prayed for pardon." Mrs. S. C. to John Wesley, May 17, 1758, in *Arminian Magazine* 4:668–669. Historian Earl Kent Brown attributes these letters to Sarah Crosby. Earl Kent Brown, *Women of Mr. Wesley's Methodism* (New York: Edwin Mellen Press, 1983), 169–170.

19. Crosby to Wesley, in *Holy Women*, 2:33. The quoted hymn is the final two lines from Charles Wesley's Redemption Hymns, hymn #42. Charles Wesley, *Hymns for Those that Seek and Those that have Redemption in the Blood of Jesus Christ* (London: Strahan, 1747). Text available at http://www.divinity.duke.edu/wesleyan/texts/cw_published_verse.html (accessed April 20, 2010).

At this point in the narrative, Crosby provides historical reference points writing, "this was about three years and a half after I was justified, and for the three years following, God gave me to walk in the light of his countenance."[20] This would place this experience in mid-1753, and the three years noted would end only a year before she writes of the experiences in this letter dated August 1757.

The three years of "walk[ing] in the light of his countenance" are then described in more detail. Crosby writes about an encounter that marked how she was cleansed from sin:

> It seemed now only needful for God to speak the word, and sin should be no more! Sometimes I thought he had done this; but then I feared deceiving myself, and continued to pray that he would seal me his, in the bonds of an everlasting covenant. Once, when I was kneeling down to pray, it was suggested to my soul with much power, "ask what thou wilt, and I will do it for thee." My soul was amazed, and replied, "Lord, I ask nothing in earth, or heaven, but perfect holiness;" and this I was assured I would receive. My heart seemed now to be dissolved in love; the presence of God surrounded me, and I have slept as in the arms of his love. I was fully assured that I should be finally saved; but what I wanted was, that God would shew me, whether he had taken the root of sin out of my heart, and sealed me by His Spirit.[21]

This longing for a seal of the Holy Spirit was answered in two encounters that offered confirmation that her experience was that of Christian Perfection:

> The Lord shewed me, that many things which I had thought were sins, were only temptations, and also what a little thing it was for him, to take the root of sin out of my heart. I feared to believe he had done it; but asked a token, and prayed he would stamp me with His Spirit's seal, and speak to my soul at his table; and was refreshed with these words,
>
> 'There, there we shall stand,
> With our harps in our hands,

---

20. Crosby to Wesley, in *Holy Women*, 2:33.
21. Ibid., 2:35-36.

> Interrupted no more,
> And eternally sing, and rejoice, and adore.'

> The next day I could not help believing, God had taken full possession of my heart; ... I felt my soul as a vessel emptied, but not filled. Day and night I was amazed at the blessed change my soul experienced; but I said nothing to anyone, because I was not, as yet, sure what the Lord had done for me; ... I now prayed much that God might shew me, if he had taken away the root of sin in the temptations that were past. And he shewed me as many waters cannot quench love, neither could the floods drown it; so neither had these floods of temptation he had brought me through, quenched the love he had given me to himself, for that was love that never faileth. I was now exceeding happy.... Soon after the glory of the Lord shone around me, I saw by faith the glory of God in the face of Jesus Christ.[22]

These encounters with God are examples of Crosby's experience of repeated assurance of God's transformation of her heart through direct experience of God. These encounters freed Crosby from the anxiety that accompanied her discovery of sin after justification.

Moreover, in 1773 Crosby wrote a letter to John Wesley that offers insight into her experience. The letter, as noted at the beginning of this chapter, was occasioned by his question about her spiritual experience and her opinion about Christian Perfection. He inquires, "Do you see Christian Perfection now in the same light you did Twenty or Ten Years ago? In the same that it is described in the Thoughts upon Perfection, or in the Plain Account? And do you experience *now* what you did *then?*"[23] Crosby's response (three months later in January

---

22. Crosby to Wesley, 1757, *Holy Women*, 2:38-39. Following this excerpt, there is an extended basking in God's glory recorded in the passage of Crosby's journal. The quoted hymn is the final four lines from Charles Wesley's *Watchnight Hymns*, hymn IX. Charles Wesley, *Hymns for the Watch-night* (London: Strahan, 1750). Text available at http://www.divinity.duke.edu/wesleyan/texts/cw_published_verse.html (accessed April 20, 2010). Interestingly, this same hymn was published in *Hymns and Sacred Poems* (1747) Hymn XVII, but the word order in the quoted line was changed from "shall we" to "we shall" for the publication of the separate volume of *Watchnight Hymns*. Crosby's quote is consistent with the wording published in the second publication. See no. 94 of *Hymns and Sacred Poems* available at the above online source.

23. Wesley to Crosby, in "John Wesley and Sarah Crosby," 80. Frank Baker published this letter from Sarah Crosby's letterbook where she preserved this inquiry, her response and Wesley response to her.

1773) is a lengthy letter written after having taken the time to read Wesley's *Plain Account* and reflect on her experience. She writes,

> In answer to your question, dear Sir, whether I now experience what I did then? I freely acknowledge I have not uninterruptedly enjoyed so great a degree of the glorious liberty wherewith Christ made me free sixteen years past, as I did then.[24]

The hindsight of her spiritual ups and downs, yet with peace that endured, allowed Crosby to interpret her experiences in the mid-1750s as the hinge point that set her free.

Thirty years later another letter used the aid of hindsight to express Crosby's confidence in her experience of Christian Perfection. Crosby (now in her 70s and in failing health) reflects back on her life and her decades of ministry in a letter to her friend, Mrs. Holder. She writes, "my soul is enabled to triumph in [Christ's] great salvation, but the worn out body will not keep pace with the spirit; it will not be always so, we shall have bodies fashioned like unto his glorious body!"[25] We see here how Crosby is thankful for the freedom that she experienced through sanctification in her lifetime, receiving the great salvation. Yet, she is not fully satisfied, and longs for even greater promises of glory after death.

Sarah Crosby's Transmission of Perfection Through Narrative

In Sarah Crosby's story I see the power of narrative to transmit the idea of Perfection in both how she received the idea and how she spread the gospel with her own story. Returning to the beginning of Crosby's story, in the 1750s she first heard about the idea of Perfection while reading John Wesley's sermons. She was not extraordinarily moved when she first heard him preach in person, but she did remember one phrase he said: "If it be possible for God to give us a little love, is it not possible for him to fill us with love?"[26] This rhetorical question is full of promise. The question relies on the evidence found in personal narrative — that God can fill people with a little love. This is

---

24. Crosby to Wesley, in *Early Methodist Spirituality*, 267.
25. Sarah Crosby to Mary Holder, Leeds, February 14, 1801, in *Holy Women*, 2:106.
26. Crosby to Wesley, in *Holy Women*, 2:28 (second page 28). Crosby to Wesley, in *Early Methodist Spirituality*, 265. Amusingly, Crosby doesn't hesitate to tell John Wesley in these letters that she did not find him a moving preaching when she first heard him. One can imagine it was a joke between friends that communicates the level of comfort between Crosby and Wesley.

evidence of God is found in the narratives of the people, rather than evidence found in an abstract theological concept. This powerful question impacted Crosby so deeply that it became a part of her spiritual narrative and is included in two different accounts of her spiritual journey.[27]

In the seasons of revival and consolidation of Methodism, many people entered the Methodist community seeking assurance of forgiveness or a conversion experience; in contrast, Crosby entered into the Methodist community already converted and intrigued with John Wesley's teaching on Christian Perfection. Crosby sought out teaching on this idea of Perfection, but her concern was less about the doctrinal details but rather whether it was possible in her own life. Interestingly, in this search she was ministered to by both Charles and John Wesley in person and through their writing.[28] With the hope of transformation Crosby joined the Methodist society and received the sign of membership, her ticket, from John Wesley himself.[29] Interacting relationally with the Methodists in class and band (the system of discipleship within the Methodist structure) now served as the vehicle for pursuing perfection and Crosby expected that this transformation could not be far away.[30] Reading John Wesley's sermon on the doctrine was instrumental in her struggle toward Perfection. She writes, "I now read Mr. J. Wesley's Sermon on *Christian Perfection,* and was convinced if this were what he meant by *perfection,* God could and would make me thus perfect; but I felt much need of that faith and patience which inherit the promises."[31] Gradually, Crosby began to believe change was possible. In her 1773 letter to Wesley, Crosby contrasts her reaction to hearing that first preached sermon with her later response to reading Wesley's sermon on Christian Perfection. She writes,

> I often thought of the only words I remembered in your sermon, the first time I heard you which were, 'If it is possible for God to give us a little love, is it not possible for him to fill us with love?' I then answered in my heart, 'Yes, it is possible, but he won't do it.' But now my language was changed, and I often said, Lord it is possible, O! that you would fill my soul with love.[32]

---

27. Crosby to Wesley, in *Holy Women*, 2:28 (second page 28). Crosby to Wesley, in *Early Methodist Spirituality*, 265.

28. Crosby to Wesley, in *Holy Women*, 2:29 (second page 29), 33.

29. Crosby to Wesley, in *Early Methodist Spirituality*, 265. See also Crosby, *Holy Women*, 2:29 (second 29).

30. Crosby to Wesley, in *Early Methodist Spirituality*, 265.

31. Crosby to Wesley, in *Holy Women*, 2:29 (second 29).

Both hearing the preaching of the Wesleys and personal interactions with the Methodist society were essential elements of how Crosby received the doctrine of Christian Perfection. Moreover, her own experience of longing to be filled with love shaped how she received John and Charles Wesley's teaching on Christian Perfection.

As seen above, Crosby entered into the Methodist society seeking after Perfection. Looking back she describes her entrance into the Methodist society like this: "O blessed time never to be forgotten by me. I now expected soon to be filled with pure love."[33] Crosby did experience God in intimate ways that filled her with love in response to this longing, although, as seen above, rather than being filled immediately in one encounter, these experiences were spread over the years to come.

During the 1760s, the multitude of Perfection narratives in Methodist communities brought about controversy as well as further nuance to the experience. Members looked to each other for cues about what could be expected in the experience of Perfection. Sarah Crosby was living with Sarah Ryan as they laboured together at Leytonstone at the Methodist orphanage. Ryan also had a Perfection experience, and Crosby compared her experience with that of her friend's. As time went on, Ryan's experience seemed to continue when Crosby's appeared to be faltering. In 1765 John Wesley wrote to encourage Crosby not to limit her expectation of Perfection to the same experience that Ryan had:

> But whatever you find now, beware you do not deny what you had once received. I do not say "a divine assurance that you should *never sin*, or sustain any *spiritual loss.*" I know not that ever you received this; but you certainly were *saved from sin*; and that as clearly, and in as high a degree as ever Sally [Sarah] Ryan was. And if you have sustained any loss in this, believe, and be made whole.[34]

In this letter, written about a decade after Crosby's experiences of God explored above, Wesley offers the corrective that Crosby's encounter with God (which freed her from sin) did not guarantee that she would be free of all future sin. In addition, John Wesley's understanding of the Christian journey allowed for loss of spiritual gains. Thus, while an experience of Christian Perfection

---

32. Crosby to Wesley, in *Early Methodist Spirituality*, 265.
33. Ibid.
34. John Wesley to Sarah Crosby, Kingswood, October 5, 1765, in *Holy Women*, 2:52. See also same letter in Wesley, *Letters*, 4:312-313. Emphasis in the original.

makes a significant impact on the believer and often lays the foundation for further growth, it also includes the possibility of future spiritual loss. As seen above, Sarah Crosby affirms the forward and backward movement in her own experience in her 1773 letter to John Wesley. In addition, in the 1773 letter she reframes her own interpretation of the season of doubt as a time when she valued the opinion of Sarah Ryan too highly and lost confidence in her experience of freedom, while freedom indeed prevailed.[35]

Looking to others and receiving inspiration from their experience of God is important for the transmission of Christian Perfection as an ideal of Christian maturity. Yet, each Perfection narrative shows a unique experience and spiritual journey. The corrective offered by Wesley in his letter to Crosby offers the interpretation that not all aspects of one Methodist's narrative can be generalized to all Perfection experiences.

In addition to narrative reception of the doctrine of Perfection, Crosby's ministry to others shows how she transmitted the doctrine of Perfection to others using narrative. Crosby's preaching ministry started through public prayer and sharing her experience of God. Also, after her death, the published narrative of her life transmitted her experiences to an even wider audience. The circulation of the *Methodist Magazine* could reach even more people than she could minister to in person. I can imagine that the people reading the *Methodist Magazine* were inspired to long for Christian Perfection as she did.

Crosby's ministry used narrative, transmitting Christian Perfection as she shared her experiences with others. In 1761 Crosby relocated to Derby where they needed a leader. She met with the class meeting of about twenty-five people one week, and then an unexpected crowd of two hundred arrived the next week looking for spiritual guidance.[36] Her journal entry for that day reads:

> Sunday [February] 8th [1781]. This day my mind has been calmly stayed on God. In the evening I expected to meet about thirty persons in class; but to my great surprise there came near two hundred; I found an awful, loving sense of the Lord's presence; but was much affected both in body and mind. I was not sure whether it was right for me to exhort in so public a manner, and yet I saw it impracticable to meet all these people by way of speaking particularly to each individual [the role of a class leader], therefore gave out a hymn and prayed, and told them part of what the Lord had done for myself, persuading them to flee from all sin.[37]

35. Crosby to Wesley, in *Early Methodist Spirituality*, 267.
36. Crosby, *Holy Women*, 2:42.

Crosby shared her personal experience as an exhortation for others to seek God. In response to this surprising development John Wesley encouraged Crosby, and other female leaders, to similarly share their experiences with Methodist gatherings with humility.[38] Crosby's ministry was extensive as she shared her narrative. Exhortations from experience eventually evolved into preaching from a text, which had been forbidden at first.[39] A great portion of the impact of Crosby's ministry, and the ministry of other local leaders — both male and female — was based on sharing personal experiences that inspire faith in God and model holiness of life. For Crosby, this sharing happened in large groups (as seen above) and in small class and band settings, sharing with a few people at a time.[40]

Another interesting aspect of Crosby's narrative ministry is that she noticed the positive impact of publicly being thankful for God's gift of Christian Perfection, particularly when testimony to this blessing is missing. Crosby notes in her diary on November 1, 1773 her conviction about the importance of sharing her spiritual experience:

> While conversing with some friends, I found a persuasion which has lately rested on my mind, much increased, namely, that though we had prayed much for blessings, we had not praised God as we ought to have done, for those which he had conferred on us, and in particular, we were all made sensible we had not borne testimony simply and plainly, at all proper times, to the great salvation God had wrought in us; nor praised him for it, as was our duty to do; and that, therefore, we had sometimes suffered loss in our souls.[41]

---

37. Ibid.

38. John Wesley to Sarah Crosby, London, February 14, 1761, in *Holy Women*, 43. See the same later also in Wesley, *Letters*, 4:133.

39. The argument for female Methodist preachers offered by Taft in the whole of *Holy Women* was supported by the narrative of Sarah Crosby's increasing role as preacher. Support includes letters from John Wesley with his advice for Crosby; and her own journal of travel and ministry document the growing acceptance of the role of female preachers over the years. See *Holy Women*, 2:42-89.

40. For example, a common description of Crosby's day of ministry is "June 14th [1774]. I met their little select band at five, and had a public meeting at seven; I went to church at one, and had a good lovefeast at five, which lasted till near eight; many spoke and my Lord opened my mouth also; I found it a good time. Glory be to God. I held a public meeting at eight. — I had a close conversation with J.B. I believe his heart is better than his head." Crosby, *Holy Women*, 2:86. See also page 2:89 for a numerical accounting of her extensive meetings in 1777.

41. Crosby, *Holy Women*, 2:59.

Crosby's worry that not enough people were witnessing to the great salvation (that is, Perfection) assumes the impact of sharing such testimony would be effective in blessing those who heard the witness. Seen here is Crosby's belief that simple praise for the blessing of her spiritual experience of Christian Perfection should and could evoke spiritual growth in others.

I imagine that the far-ranging exhorting and preaching ministry of Sarah Crosby resulted in many who heard her story and were provoked to their own experience of God. The records in Crosby's journal of her travels and ministry include regular evaluation of the meetings as "good" or "affecting." In addition to these general comments, there is evidence of the transmission of the doctrine of Christian Perfection by sharing her own spiritual experience. On Tuesday, April 25, 1774 she writes,

> Glory be to thy name, O let the bread cast upon the waters be found after many days; but blessed be my Lord, some is found already, for several have joined in society, who were blessed in my meetings on Sunday; some were set at liberty, and two were blessed with perfect love.[42]

This journal entry does not offer details of the content of what was shared: was it her conversion experience, her experience of suffering or possibly her experience of Christian Perfection? It is, however, an example of how Crosby's ministry, often composed of sharing her spiritual experience, was effective in evoking an experience of Christian Perfection in others.

Sarah Crosby and Longing for Perfection

It has been shown how Sarah Crosby experienced God in her own life, and how the idea of Perfection was transmitted through her. In addition, more can be learned about other elements of the doctrine of Perfection from looking more closely at how Crosby embodied the doctrine of Christian Perfection. In particular, Crosby's narrative illustrates an intense longing for the experience of Perfection.

Sarah Crosby experienced longing for God following her conversion, longing for a holy life for the purpose of being acceptable in the eyes of God. More and more after her assurance of forgiveness Crosby increased in self-knowledge, yet this increase only revealed the depth of her sinful heart.[43] When

---

42. Ibid., 2:84.
43. Ibid., 2:31.

the increased knowledge of herself failed to result in Perfection, Crosby sought more knowledge of God and His love as the avenue to the pure love that would cleanse from the evil tempers of her heart. She writes, "I was now convinced that I had hitherto sought *knowledge*, more than the *love of God,* which error I prayed God to forgive, promising I would now seek his love alone."[44] In seeking after God's love Crosby found an endless source which she would long for more and more throughout her life.

After the experiences surveyed above that cleansed her from sin and filled her with love, she longed for more of God. In her journal on May 22, 1763 she writes,

> I am not, indeed, torn by wrong tempers, or sinful desires; in this respect I have rest; and not only in this: for my confidence in the Lord is strong, and increaseth daily, as also my love to him and his dear children; but I have one want, one desire, which is yet unsatisfied, and that is, that I may always live in the spirit and mind of Jesus.[45]

She goes on to describe what the mind of Christ is that she longs for:

> O who can conceive the degree of mildness his precious heart felt to poor sinners, or the tenderness of love that melted his breast toward his own people; or the fervency of delight he enjoyed in communion with his heavenly Father; O Jesus, explain this to my heart![46]

Here, for Crosby, the mind of Christ is marked by compassion for others and intimate relationship with God the Father. It is this ideal for which she is longs.

A few months later, on August 8, 1763, Crosby longs for more holiness as the result of God's presence in her life. She writes,

> What great mercy has thou shewed me this month past! Thou has often taken me into thy banqueting house, and thy banner over me has been love. Now I sit under thy shadow with great delight. O blessed Jesus! thou hast also greatly humbled me before thee, give me to remember my past sins and follies.
>
>   'May I this life improve

---

44. Ibid., 2:33.
45. Ibid., 2:50.
46. Ibid.

> To mourn for follies past;
> And live this short revolving day,
> As if it were my last.'

> This thou knowest is the one desire of my heart. O what has thou done for me! What a great deliverance has thou wrought! Lord, make me pure, spiritual, holy. Mould as thou wilt the passive clay. Sweetly and quietly to live in thy will, and prove that God, my God is love, is my request. Wilt thou not grant it? Lord increase my faith.[47]

Here Crosby tells of her encounter with God, her awareness of her sinfulness and her longing for more holiness. This is an example of spirituality that is shaped by the Methodist understanding of Christian maturity as Christian Perfection, and continued growth in grace. Crosby's intense experiences of God evoked humble longing for even more holiness, which produced a dynamic movement toward God, not a static state of Perfection that does not grow deeper.

Furthermore, in old age Crosby longed for more of God Himself. In her journal on June 3, 1800, at the age of 70 she writes, "I have enjoyed many reviving seasons for these last few months, blessed be my Lord. But I long for deeper manifestations of the divine nature. O, when shall I be overwhelmed with thy delightful presence."[48] There is none of the concern for having lost spiritual advancement that John Wesley corrected in the younger Crosby. Here there is only longing for more of her Saviour's love and more of God.

Crosby ministered in many communities, even right up to her death just before her seventy-fifth birthday. Her friend, Anne Tripp, recorded the last days of her life, noting that despite poor health Crosby attended worship and a select band meeting. Crosby's words in the final days confirmed her deep assurance that God is good, and that she would meet him soon. Crosby touched many lives during her life, and the publication of her memoir in the *Methodist Magazine* came in response to the request to the editor for the readers to be inspired by Crosby's life experiences.[49] In the final days Crosby received the assuring words from God: "I will never leave thee."[50] Her life of faith reflects that she lived out that same promise to God.

---

47. Ibid., 2:51.
48. Ibid., 2:107.
49. Mrs. E. Mortimer to the editor of the *Methodist Magazine*, Islington, January 7, 1806, in *Methodist Magazine*, 29 (1806) 418. Also in *Holy Women*, 2:25.
50. Letter from Trip, in *Holy Women*, 2:113-114.

The story of Sarah Crosby offers witness of a faithful and honest early Methodist life and demonstrates four aspects of the experience of Christian Perfection. First, she shows us the joy of conversion and how honest reflection reveals sin after conversion. Second, how faith in the transforming power of God's love released her from the grip of inbred sin such as anger and self-will. Third, Crosby's passion is ignited to love others and share her narrative when she received love from God. Fourth, she embodies Perfection and shows the perseverance and longing for more of God that is evoked when she was given a taste of the Divine presence in her experience of Christian Perfection.

Finally, in the sources for Sarah Crosby's life, there are clues as to how her idea of Perfection was shaped by the narrative of others. Her desire for Perfection was spurred on by meeting in class with other believers seeking the same thing; and she passed on this concept of Christian Perfection through her own ministry. The doctrine of Christian Perfection was passed on through the publication of her written accounts, and powerfully through personal encounters and her own life of holiness.

7

George Clark and the Transformed Life

> It is not a little thing to give up the heart to the Lord, so as to let him cleanse it and make it a presence-chamber for himself.
> — George Clark, *Arminian Magazine*, 1790[1]

In a letter to John Wesley on July 29, 1774 George Clark (1710-1797) writes,

> Less than thirty years ago I was an entire stranger to heart Religion; but by hearing you preach, and by receiving the Truth in love, an entire change took place ... I believed the doctrine of entire Sanctification, I prayed, and lived in hope: and the Lord who saw my desire granted my request. For on the 30th of May, 1762, my soul was set at liberty.[2]

Eight years after this letter was written, in June of 1782 John Wesley started publishing extracts from the journal of George Clark in the *Arminian Magazine*.[3] John Wesley introduced the extracts by commending the journal to the reader and describing the selection of extracts as those

> which artlessly describe the struggle between the flesh and the Spirit, even in a true Believer; and those which relate to the accomplishment of that grand Promise, which is the Quintessence of the Gospel, 'I will circumcise thy heart, to love the Lord thy God with all thy heart, and with all thy soul.'[4]

---

1. George Clark, "Thoughts on the Work of Sanctification," in *Arminian Magazine* 13(1790) 45.
2. Mr. G. Clark to John Wesley, London, July 29, 1774, in *Arminian Magazine* 10 (1787) 103-104.
3. George Clark, "An Extract from the Journal of Mr. G— C—," in *Arminian Magazine*, 5 (1782)298-301, 351-355, 404-408, 465-468, 519-524, 575-580, 639-641; 6 (1783)19-22, 73-76, 125-127, 186-189, 244-246, 299-302, 352-355, 407-410, 464-468.

Wesley used the powerful narrative of a man known in the Methodist community to illustrate Christian Perfection. Clark's example illustrates the reality of the believer's struggle with sin after justification, and the hope of success in this struggle. His life story — both raw and honest — is an embodiment of the goal of seeking after holiness. His story provides inspiration for seeking a life of holiness, not only because Clark is honest about his struggle with sin, but also because of the transformation of his life after his experience of Christian Perfection.

The sources of information regarding the life of George Clark are limited. There are significant journal extracts published in the *Arminian Magazine*.[5] A letter from Clark is published in the *Arminian Magazine* in 1787 and also a short theological treatise on sanctification reflects theologically on the Perfectionist controversy in London in the 1760s.[6] There are two references to Clark in John Wesley's collected letters;[7] and the final artefact regarding this early Methodist man is a gravestone which records his death date as May 14, 1797.[8]

George Clark's Story

George Clark was born July 1, 1710 in a British colony, the Province of New York, while his father was governor there. As a child he travelled to London with his mother to return to her home.[9] His mother was the daughter of a London merchant, and later in his journal Clark mentions that his estranged father was a gentleman.[10] He tells of a poverty stricken childhood that separated him from his mother. He lived wildly and without the influence of religion, yet even with this lifestyle he notes a period when he was blessed by the act of daily prayer.[11] Clark married at the age of twenty-five and soon took over the newspaper business of his wife's late father.[12] After illness and financial struggle,

---

4. Wesley, *Arminian Magazine*, 5:298-301. Also consider the editor's comments at the end of the journal excerpts, Arminian Magazine 6:468.

5. Clark, Arminian Magazine, 6:19. See the Appendix for more detailed information about the sources.

6. Clark to Wesley, in Arminian Magazine 10:103-105. The letter indicates the same author as the journal with the mention of a Perfection experience on the same day. Clark, *Arminian Magazine*, 13:42-45. For more on the Perfectionist controversy, see chapter 1, pages 11-12.

7. John Wesley to Jonah Freeman, December 20, 1762, in *Letters*, 4:197. John Wesley to Mary Bosanquet, in *Letters*, 7:43.

8. George John Stevenson, *City Chapel Road, London, and its Associations, Historical, Biographical, and Memorial* (London: George J. Stevenson, 1872), 506-507.

9. Clark, *Arminian Magazine*, 5:298.

10. Ibid., 5:298, 6:73.

11. Ibid., 5:299.

Clark outwardly reformed from earlier patterns allowing him to work and care for his family, but he still had no religion in his life. Clark suffered a significant loss when his wife died of consumption and soon after their two children died of small-pox. This left Clark caring for his wife's daughter from a previous relationship and both his own mother and his wife's mother.[13]

On the insistence of his mother, Clark heard John Wesley preach. He slowly warmed up to the Methodist community, joining the Methodist society in November 1746. His commitment to this voluntary society at that time was centred on the rules established for membership in the society. He was inspired by the rules and attempted to keep them by his own resolve.[14] His attendance in the society caused increased spiritual awakening over the next months until February 15, 1747 when something new happened:

> That morning I found a strange alteration. I felt no more condemnation. I had liberty to pray, and a full assurance, that my prayer was heard. Yet this was but as a drop before a shower. For at the Chapel the love of God so over-powered me, that I could not bear up under the weight of it, but was obliged to sit or kneel [a] great part of the service. ... My soul had now a clear sense of its union with Jesus. And I peculiarly loved him.[15]

This account of his conversion ends the first excerpt of the published journal and sets the stage for Clark's lifelong journey toward holiness.

The struggle with sin after conversion dominates Clark's journal. In an account before the dated journal entries begin, Clark notes that after his conversion he expected to be free from sin, particularly anger. When anger remained, his peace and communion with Christ were disturbed and he began to sense the depth of his sinfulness. A fluctuation between feeling sinful and feeling God's love characterized Clark's spirituality for decades. Fortunately, the persistent doubt and fear that surfaced after his initial conversion experience were lifted after about two years and he felt a new freedom to live day by day. The result of this freedom was to begin recording God's dealing with his soul in his journal. The journal records striving for faithful living, experiences of peace and joy in the presence of God, and increasing awareness of the depth of sin as he struggled with pride, anger, self-will and unbelief.[16] These inward

---

12. Ibid., 5:300.
13. Ibid.
14. Ibid., 5:301.
15. Ibid.

attitudes expressed themselves in everyday ways: he notes struggles with anger as he raised his wife's daughter as his own;[17] he experienced the humbling of pride in his work as a porter;[18] and as a widower, he struggled to have chaste, yet meaningful relationships with women.[19]

The journal entry for November 17, 1757 offers a window into Clark's pious activity. He writes,

> Is not this a token, that I shall overcome my evil heart at last, that I am seldom turned aside from prayer? I constantly open the secrets of my soul to the Lord, and am hereby strengthened to endure and to conquer. Indeed I find great help in the means, particularly my Band and Class; for which I cannot sufficiently bless God.[20]

The pious activities themselves did not produce the purity he sought, but through them he was prepared to be transformed.

After fifteen years of struggle, Clark had a transforming encounter with God on Pentecost Sunday, May 30, 1762. In the midst of public worship after reflecting on the Holy Spirit's descent on the disciples on Pentecost he states that the "Spirit made me deeply sensible of his presence."[21] As quoted in the introduction, here is Clark's narrative in his own words:

> I then pleaded with him, and that with many tears, to make me a partaker of his sanctifying love, by removing forever the bitter root of pride, self-will and unbelief. All this time my heart was broken before the Lord, and my face covered with tears: and I found nothing left but a fear lest the Spirit should depart, before he had purified me from inbred sin. While I was thus agonizing with God in prayer, the power of the Lord came upon me, so that my whole body trembled under it. But I kept my spirit still, and continually cried, 'My heart, Lord! work within! work within!' In that instant I felt the Spirit of God enter into my heart with mighty power, and as it were literally accomplish that promise, *I will take away the heart of stone, and give*

---

16. See Clark, *Arminian Magazine*, 5:405, 467 for examples of his awareness of these inward sins.
17. Ibid., 5:465, 467.
18. Ibid., 5:579.
19. For examples, see the entry for January 19, 1757, Ibid., 5:639-640. Or the entry for April 23, June 1, July 11 1760, idem., 6;73-75. Or the entries December 24, 1760 to February 15, 1761, idem., 6:125-127.
20. Ibid., 5:641.
21. Ibid., 6:245.

you a heart of flesh: the old heart seeming to be taken away, and God himself taking possession of my soul in the fulness of love: and all the time of the service, I enjoyed such a heaven of love as I never before experienced. All the day I watched every motion of my heart, to see if the evils I before felt were there or not: but I found none: I could find nothing there, but solid joy and heart-felt peace.[22]

Clark had finally found the freedom from sin he had been seeking.

Clark's life was transformed by the ecstatic encounter with God that he had on Pentecost Sunday. The tone of the journal changes dramatically after this event. The guilt and shame over anger and pride are gone. He is humble and thankful for his continued peace with God, and his concern shifts to other people.[23]

Soon after his Perfection narrative, Clark began to express particular concern for a group within the Methodist society in London. He wrote of increasing pride among some in the society, particularly that they thought of themselves as higher than their teachers.[24] As the story unfolds, the details correlate with the events in London surrounding the Perfectionist controversy (described in chapter one).[25] He recorded on June 7, 1763 that there was a plan to separate, a plan fuelled by pride in those who planned to leave.[26] By September 14 of that same year, he reported that nearly two hundred had left, and the impact on those that remained was significant. While the comments generally were vague, in one entry Clark noted particularly that the controversy tarnished the doctrine of Christian Perfection.[27]

The conclusion to Clark's story is found in the final two published excerpts spanning many years. The entries reflect deteriorating health, and increasing faith and holiness. Clark was moving deeper and deeper into the love and peace of God.[28] The journal was published while Clark was still living, therefore it

---

22. Ibid., 6:245.
23. Ibid., 6:299.
24. See the entries for Dec 9, 1762 and Jan 14, 1763, ibid., 6:299. Idem., 6:300.
25. For more on the Perfectionist controversy, see pages 11-12 in chapter one. Interestingly, Charles Goodwin refers to the event in London at this time as the "London Blessing," Charles H. Goodwin, "Setting Perfection too High: John Wesley's Changing Attitudes Toward the 'London Blessing'," *Methodist History* 36, no. 2 (January 1998): 86-96. A letter from John Wesley to Jonah Freeman is addressed to him: "at Mr. Clark's, Hosier, In Farr's Alley, Aldersgate Street" and dated December 20, 1762. This places Clark in London during the time period of the Perfectionist controversy. *Letters*, 4:197.
26. Clark, *Arminian Magazine*, 6:301.
27. Ibid., 6:302.
28. Ibid., 6:352, 408.

does not offer the full conclusion to his story which came on May 14, 1797 when he passed away after a long life in the service of God by serving the Methodist communities in London.[29]

George Clark's Transmission of Christian Perfection through Narrative

The published journal of George Clark was part of John Wesley's effort to spread the idea of Christian Perfection using the power of narrative. It was published in the *Arminian Magazine* for the purpose of setting Clark up as an exemplar.[30] In addition, the narrative shows the influence of story and community on Clark's understanding of Perfection. He sat under teaching that inspired him to seek Perfection, and he rejected contrary teaching, namely that Perfection could not be reached until death.[31] He was inspired by meeting people who were blessed to have been released from the struggle with inbred sin that he was also fighting.[32] Moreover, he saw with distaste the character of those who followed skewed teaching on Perfection and this corrected and nuanced his own theology.

The story of Perfection began for George Clark on May 12, 1757, years before his own Perfection narrative. Clark writes,

> I was in company with some who feel nothing contrary to love, and who have constant communion with God. Hereby my hope was much strengthened of an entire deliverance from sin, that I might be truly holy, totally renewed in the image of my mind, by the powerful working of the Spirit of Jesus.[33]

Although Clark had been seeking deliverance from sin for most of the ten years since his conversion experience, this encounter with transformed people reinforced the hope of freedom from his struggle with inbred sin (such as pride and anger). It is noteworthy that he described the people he met by the characteristics they had: that they had love and communion with God. This is an example of how narrative can establish a vision of what to seek. Also interesting is that Clark placed his hope for transformation on God's power, not

---

29. Stevenson, *City Chapel Road*, 506.
30. Clark, *Arminian Magazine*, 5:298-301, 6:468.
31. Ibid., 6:186-187, 6:301, 6:353, 6:466.
32. Ibid., 5:640, 6:246.
33. Ibid., 5:640.

on his own ability to resist temptation. Clark saw that Perfection was a gift from God, not attained by human effort.

In addition to hearing a narrative of Perfection, Clark briefly records another encouraging encounter. Less than a month after his experience of Perfection he writes, "I had much comfort and instruction from one that has long enjoyed the great Salvation."[34] In the weeks between his experience of Perfection and this entry, Clark struggled with the temptation to doubt his experience. Amidst the struggle, is this encounter with another believer who shared his experience, particularly one who had enjoyed the lasting effects. This encounter provided significant encouragement to Clark. This example illustrates the ongoing role that sharing narrative had in his continued spiritual growth after his Perfection experience.

The impact of narrative to encourage Clark toward Perfection was contrasted with the presence of counter-narratives in his life. About one year before his experience of Perfection, he remarks in his journal about an encounter with friends who advised against expecting instantaneous Perfection. On June 28, 1761 he writes,

> Some of my friends tell me, 'It cannot be: that there is no instantaneous work after Justification: but only a gradual decay of sin.' When I give way to this, I suffer much loss: I lose all my hunger and thirst after righteousness. And I see those who are of this opinion gain no ground, but are just what they were twenty years ago.[35]

The effort of his friends had the opposite of the intended effect. They affirmed Clark's pursuit of Perfection as he saw their own narratives develop into lives in a way he did not wish to emulate.

Similarly, two years later on the one year anniversary of his experience of Perfection, Clark reflects on how he rejected the teaching noted above. He writes,

> This day I was delivered from the corruption of my nature. How wanting to themselves are they, who being justified, yet do not believe so as to enjoy that pure and holy Love, which cleanses from all sin? What a loss had I sustained, had I believed those who said, "Death only could save from inbred sin?["][36]

---

34. Ibid., 6:246.
35. Ibid., 6:186-187.
36. Ibid., 6:301.

In hindsight, Clark was glad for his persistence against the narrative offered by the alternative theological position. Ironically, the narrative of those who did not agree with Christian Perfection impacted Clark for the good in his pursuit of holiness.

About this time, another group of people reinforced Clark's idea of Perfection through their counter-narrative: those who broke with the Methodists in London during the Perfectionist controversy. In 1763 in particular Clark makes multiple comments about those who were separating from Methodist fellowship.[37] His observations include reflections on the lack of humility on the part of those who claim Perfection and the presence of pride undermined the influence of their counter-narrative of Perfection. On June 7, 1763 he writes,

> For several days I have been in pain for our mistaken brethren, who resolve to separate from us, "Because (they say) we have not the faith and love which they have." If it were so, they should stay and help us to attain to it. But the truth is, they think too highly of themselves. And I fear, this will greatly hinder the work which God is so powerfully carrying on among us.[38]

Similar to those who influenced Clark to pursue Perfection, these people claimed an experience of God that brought transformation in their life. Yet, the pride of their conduct brought Clark pain and provoked him to prayer, rather than commending their teaching on Perfection.

Further insight into the break in fellowship in London is offered in the theological reflections in "Thoughts on the Work of Sanctification" by Mr. G. C. From the similarity of perspective it is likely that this is the same G. C. as the journal, that is George Clark. Clark reflects that the pride of those who left the Methodist fellowship in London was based on the belief that once perfected they could not sin. He writes,

> They said, if any, who had received that grace [being cleansed from all sin], said they could lose it, they had not received the gift they had. Here commenced the work of the devil, who made them believe what they really said; That they were more holy than our first parents, and stood on a better foundation.[39]

---

37. Ibid., 6:299-301.
38. Ibid., 6:301.

Here Clark cites pride, so much so that this group thought themselves better than Adam and Eve, able to resist any future sin.[40] Interestingly, pride itself is one of the key inbred sins that Clark struggled with after justification but before Perfection.[41] While accusations of pride often become self-condemning for the accuser in light of their own pride, it is not so with Clark for his journal reflects growing humility. Clark's ideas were shaped by those who claimed Perfection in London in the 1760s. These claims alongside his own experience of transformation shaped his theology of Perfection. From this example it is seen that narratives that claim an experience of Perfection, such as the Perfectionists claimed, are not enough to evoke emulation. Narratives of Perfection that had real impact to spread the doctrine from person to person were supported by narratives of transformed lives.

In addition to receiving the idea of Christian Perfection by narrative, Clark participated in the Methodist practice of sharing his narrative. Because of his involvement in the Methodist society in London, I can imagine that Clark told his story to various small groups, such as at band and class meetings. Moreover, only one week after his Perfection narrative, Clark shared at a Love-feast: "I am saved from all fear and unbelief: yet I feel myself more weak than ever; but the Lord gives a clearer and clearer light touching what he hath wrote. And this evening I spoke of it at the Love-feast, though with much trembling."[42] This journal entry is a simple acknowledgement of how Clark continued the chain of transmission of the doctrine of Perfection in the Methodist community. Furthermore, the letter written to John Wesley that is quoted at the beginning of this chapter shows that this was not the last time Clark shared what God did in his life on Pentecost Sunday in 1762.

George Clark and the Transformative Power of Perfection

---

39. Clark, "Thoughts," in *Arminian Magazine*, 13:42. See also Mr. J.B. "Thoughts on Perfection," in *Arminian Magazine*, 4:549-553. This short piece also suggests similar ideas to those Clark puts forward.

40. John Wesley's teaching on Perfection never claimed the ability of Christian Perfection to prevent all future sin. Those who had an experience of Perfection were able to lose what they had attained and were in as much need of God's continued grace as any other believer. About this same time in "Cautions and Directions Given to the Greatest Professors in The Methodist Societies" (1762), Wesley warns against this misplaced expectation that they cannot sin. Wesley, "Cautions and Directions Given to the Greatest Professors in The Methodist Societies," in *John Wesley*, 305.

41. Clark, *Arminian Magazine*, 5:352, 405, 467, 579. Also compare Sarah Crosby's identification of pride among her sins. Taft, *Holy Women*, 2:31. See also John Wesley's list of inbred sins in his sermon, "The Repentance of Believers," Wesley, Sermon 14, "Repentance", in §I.3-4 in *Works*, 1:337.

42. Clark, *Arminian Magazine*, 6:245-246.

George Clark, reflecting on the change that had occurred in his life after his Perfection experience writes, "I am called to live by faith in a manner I never saw before. My soul now naturally cleaves to Jesus."[43] The transformative power of the experience of Perfection is represented in the journal excerpts as a sharp contrast before and after the experience. There is a shift in tone after his Perfection experience on May 30, 1762, moving from fear and doubt to peace and humility. Thus, Clark's story embodies the power of Perfection to transform a life.

The transformative power of Clark's Perfection experience is in the context of the larger Wesleyan Methodist understanding of the Christian life.[44] Looking at Clark's story from the beginning, it is clear that prior to his Perfection experience, his conversion enabled transformation in outward ways, bringing Clark into community and accountability in the Methodist society in London.[45] After his conversion, Clark went through the struggle which John Wesley teaches believers to expect: the struggle with doubt, temptation and sin after conversion. After Clark was converted and the outward behaviour of his life began to change, he became more aware of the inbred sin that plagued him. After his conversion pride, self-will, anger and doubt were the repeated manifestations of inbred sin.[46]

The increasing awareness of sin is a mark of the early journal entries. For example, on February 9, 1753 he writes,

> yesterday and to-day I have felt much grief of heart, and many tears have I shed, at feeling the strength of my corrupt nature. Unbelief also prevails over me, and fear that I shall not hold out to the end. This and the various temptations I feel make me so peevish, that I am a burden to myself.[47]

This struggle with sin is in contrast to days of feeling overwhelmed by the love of God.[48] Clark even felt both sin and the presence of God at the same time:

---

43. Ibid., 6:246.

44. For more on the Wesleyan Methodist way of salvation, see the chapter two.

45. Clark, *Arminian Magazine*, 5:301.

46. Compare Sarah Crosby's identification of pride, anger and self-will as her inbred sins. Crosby, *Holy Women*, 31. Compare also John Wesley's list of inbred sins referencing pride and self-will in his sermon, "The Repentance of Believers," Wesley, *Works*, 1:337, Paragraph I.3-4.

47. Clark, *Arminian Magazine*, 5:523.

48. For example: "Sunday, Sept 10 [1756]. Inexpressible has been the painful emptiness I have found for several days past. I try my heart and my ways by the word of God, with fervent prayer, and find nothing of actual sin. But it is pride that tears me. When I have much love, I am lifted up above what I

> September 7 [1755]. I am in general very sensible of the presence of God, and afraid to sin against him. I am much in prayer, and indeed cannot live without it: it is my only refuge, I am so tempted, that I should assuredly fall, were I not continually to make my request know to God. My heart is grieved for having so long served sin, which I want to be still more penitent for. Not that I feel any guilt: that is washed away. Yet, O, I am not holy![49]

Here Clark indicates that he saw himself in a middle state after conversion (justification) but still growing in holiness (sanctification). He further notes that he was released from guilt at conversion, but that was not enough to give him the ability to resist temptation or remove inbred sin. He sought after — and expected to achieve — a life where sin held less power.

The continual oscillation between joy and temptation marks the first half of the journal excerpts published in the *Arminian Magazine*. In reading Clark's story it is wearying to watch the honest struggle. It creates a desire in the reader on behalf of Clark to find freedom. As noted above, this freedom from the struggle comes in the twelfth excerpt, on Pentecost Sunday, 1762. Throughout the service he cried out for God's presence to purify his life and fill him with love. He received what he sought and it was marked by the words of the prophet Ezekiel:

> In that instant I felt the Spirit of God enter into my heart with mighty power, and as it were literally accomplish that promise, *I will take away the heart of stone, and give you a heart of flesh*: the old heart seeming to be taken away, and God himself taking possession of my soul in the fulness of love: and all the time of the service, I enjoyed such a heaven of love as I never before experienced. All the day I watched every motion of my heart, to see if the evils I before felt were there or not: but I found none: I could find nothing there, but solid joy and heart-felt peace.[50]

---

ought to be. And when I am made to possess my own iniquity, my spirit frets against God. Yet this day has been a sabbath of rest, in which I have enjoyed much love: but I know not how to keep it." Ibid., 5:579-580.

49. Ibid., 5:578.

50. Ibid., 6:245. Allusion is to Ezekiel 11:19, or 36:26, but this reference is not word for word. Emphasis in original.

Clark had encountered God in an intense way and the encounter produced transformation. Further doubts were removed when he sought the witness to his sanctification:

> I wanted the witness of the Spirit, concerning my Sanctification, and I earnestly cried to God for it. Then were those words applied to my heart, *The weapons of our warfare are not carnal, but mighty through God to the throwing down of strong-holds, destroying reasonings, and every thing which exalteth itself against the knowledge of God, and bringing every thought into captivity to the obedience of Christ.*[51]

This encounter with God, his experience of Perfection was the turning point when Clark found the freedom from sin that he had been seeking for fifteen years.

The reader might expect that Clark's pattern would hold and the above encounter with God is one of the joy-filled days that would be followed by doubt, but that is not the case. The journal entries that follow are significantly different. For example, when struggle with doubt occurred, he framed it as Satan's attack tempting him to doubt, rather than actual doubt itself.[52] Instead of doubt and fluctuation, the journal is marked with peace and thankfulness. For example, Clark celebrated lasting peace after his experience of Christian Perfection. About a month after celebrating the one year anniversary of his experience, Clark reflects on the lasting effects writing,

> By the mercy of God, the peace and love I have enjoyed for many months does not diminish, but rather increase; though I have never had the rapturous Joy, which many have. If I had, I had probably been carried away with the same Enthusiasm. But this day my soul had a lively sense of its union with Jesus in holy love.[53]

The continued thankfulness for peace and freedom is evidence of the transformation. Yet, the experience continued to deepen. December 11, 1763 found Clark feeling "a purer love, and in a greater degree," and January 1, 1764 found Clark "preserved in perfect peace."[54] Clearly, Clark's sanctification

---

51. Ibid., 6:245. Emphasis in original.
52. Ibid., 6:245. The incident occurs only one week later on Sunday, June 6.
53. Ibid., 6:301. Clark's comment about enthusiasm is best understood when set in the historical context of the Perfectionist controversy where ecstatic encounters with God were increasing and the settled peace Clark claims was not always evident.
54. Ibid., 6:352, 353.

was not a static event. The continued growth in his life was a sign of the transformation.

Clark noted his observation of the transformation in the journal entry for June 3, 1764, two years after his experience:

> I find much peace, power, and love. As to inward conflicts, I feel them not. Yet do I never forget, that I am in the body, and continually subject to temptations, from my own ignorance and weakness. From the world and the devil, as also from weak brethren. But I find constant communion with God, and am not afraid of being overcome of evil.[55]

The peace of this description is so unlike the angst of entries noted previously. In light of the anniversary celebrations ascribing meaning to his experience, it is clear that his Perfection narrative from May 30, 1762, was the event that changed his life.[56]

The transformative change in Clark's journal embodies the doctrine of Perfection and the description of holy tempers which is presented by John Wesley. In the early journal entries Clark was longing for deliverance from temptation, yet his later entries say he was still tempted.[57] John Wesley described this type of change as transformation of the tempers, rather than expecting the absence of temptation. Holy tempers are foundational for fighting inbred sins like pride and anger. Theologian Randy Maddox draws attention to John Wesley's theological anthropology of holy tempers as fundamental to Christian Perfection. Maddox explains, "Wesley is using the term [temper] in a much broader sense than was common in the eighteenth century, where 'temper' referred to any enduring character disposition."[58] Maddox explains further that "[Wesley] frequently discussed sin in terms of a threefold division: sinful nature or tempers, sinful words, and sinful actions. The point of this division was that sinful actions and words *flow from* corrupted tempers, so the problem of sin must ultimately be addressed at this affectional level."[59] As explored in chapter two, Wesley's doctrine of Perfection allows for ignorance

---

55. Ibid., 6:353-354.

56. The entry for May 30, 1763 marks the one year anniversary, ibid., 6:301. June 30, 1764 marks the two year (plus one month) anniversary, idem., 6:354.

57. For example, see entry for June 6, 1764, ibid., 6:353.

58. Randy Maddox, "A Change of Affections: The Development, Dynamics, and Dethronement of John Wesley's 'Heart Religion'" in *"Heart Religion," in the Methodist Tradition and Related Movements*, ed. Richard Steele (Metuchen, NJ: Scarecrow Press, 2001), 15.

59. bid., 17. Emphasis in original.

and mistakes, yet still promises a life of peace and love through the means of transforming the tempers.

For example, the transformation of the tempers is seen in the contrast in journal entries before and after the Perfection narrative when Clark reflects on his unworthiness before God. On October 24, 1754 (before his Perfection account) he writes, "surely God never undertook to save so vile a wretch as me! ... O that I could leave my heart with him, who alone is able to bring a clean thing out of an unclean!"[60] Before his Perfection experience, the intensity of his self-condemnation is felt in his words (and even punctuation); but he has not fully despaired, he is still seeking Perfection.

In contrast, after his Perfection experience Clark still feels unworthy, but it is marked by humility rather than self-loathing. On January 2, 1763 he writes, "to-day I was filled with love, and deeply humbled under a sense of my unworthiness."[61] The peace that marks this entry (and other journal entries after the Perfection narrative) is expressed through the shift in the view of his unworthiness. While the unworthiness remains, Clark's attention has shifted to God and away from the struggles of his own life.

Further evidence of Clark's transformation is seen as he describes life when he celebrates the anniversary of his experience of Christian Perfection. Two years and one month after the experience he reflects in his journal on the state of his soul. He writes,

> June 30 [1764]. My soul rejoices in its deliverance from the yoke of inbred corruption. Two years have I enjoyed this Liberty, not only from the power of sin, but from unbelief, having now no shadow of a doubt, touching the accomplishment of all the promises of God. Now also my mind cleaves steadily to Jesus, without the shadow of a desire to depart from the ways of God. I find likewise an entire freedom from the works of the law: I mean, from the hope of acceptance by any thing I do, separate from my union with Christ, to whom my soul naturally cleaves in every temptation. Yet, I often weep, that I have so little love to Him, and the souls of men.[62]

---

60. Clark, *Arminian Magazine*, 5:577. Similarly on December 9, 1758 he writes, "[God] cannot endure so vile a wretch, and therefore he has left me. Yet my heart pursues him with all its strength: though that seems perfect weakness." Idem., 6:73.

61. Ibid., 6:300.

62. Ibid., 6:353.

Two years after his Perfection experience Clark remained free from the things that enslaved him: inbred corruption, unbelief, trust in the law. Instead of inbred sin, Clark's life was marked by love and peace.

The last journal entry published in the *Arminian Magazine* communicates thankfulness, this time thankfulness for twenty years of peace. Clark's words reflect the fruit of his life:

> December 1781. To this time I have not turned aside, or ceased from following the Captain of my salvation, who has led me from grace to grace, and from strength to strength, so as to go more and more out of myself, and to be fixt, for all wisdom, power and holiness, and all temporal and eternal good, on him alone. I feel the witness and the happy necessity of this every day; every fresh discovery of which unites me more unto Jesus.[63]

The transformation that occurred grew and deepened over the years and this journal entry testifies to the lasting effect of Clark's experience of Christian Perfection.

The excerpts of George Clark's journal published in the *Arminian Magazine* in 1782 and 1783 are a window into the spirituality of one Methodist man, not the most famous, nor even the most pious. His struggles and successes, joys and sorrows are enriched by the everyday-ness of living life with Christ. Clark's narrative contains evidence of the narratives around him that influenced him toward Perfection. He responded likewise by sharing his narrative personally and his story was made available to the wider community through the printed magazine. In addition, Clark's narrative has potential to continue to inspire because it is both so ordinary and yet he encountered God in extraordinary ways. Clark's narrative embodies the doctrine of Perfection by illustrating both the struggle with sin (even after conversion) as well as illustrating the transformation that is possible after an experience of Christian Perfection.

---

63. Ibid., 6:467-468.

8

William Hunter Preaching Christian Perfection

> Being thus perfected in love, we are much more qualified to grow in grace, and in the knowledge of our Lord and Saviour Jesus Christ ... O precious salvation! Let me ever be a witness of it!
>
> William Hunter to John Wesley, 1779[1]

John Wesley often lamented that the itinerant Methodist preachers did not preach his favoured doctrine of Christian Perfection as they ministered to the converts of Methodism. From the above epigraph it is obvious that lay preacher William Hunter (1728-1797), an eager advocate for Christian Perfection, was not one of the preachers of whom Wesley complained.

The story of William Hunter is among the spiritual testimonies printed in the *Arminian Magazine* by John Wesley. His witness to both conversion and Perfection was offered to the people who heard Hunter preach, but the readership of the *Arminian Magazine* provided a wider audience for his narrative.[2] Two letters were published in the *Arminian Magazine*, accompanied by a image of Hunter in the form of a woodcutting.[3]

The letters were written to John Wesley by Hunter and they form the core of the sources for the spiritual life of this lay preacher. The letters, which were solicited by Wesley, are simple and honest. In the second letter Hunter reflects on his experience of being saved from inbred sin, offering to "simply relate what I know of the dealings of God with me in this respect."[4] Yet, ever the preacher, he does offer some interpretation, not solely his story. Still, the power behind his exhortation to holiness is his narrative of experiencing Christian Perfection.

---

1. William Hunter to John Wesley, Richmond, August 29, 1779, in *The Lives of Early Methodist Preachers*. ed. Thomas Jackson, 3rd ed. (London: Wesleyan Conference Office, 1878), 2:250.
2. Hunter to Wesley, August 18, 29, 1779, in *Arminian Magazine*, 2:589-598.
3. See Appendix for more details on the sources for the life of William Hunter.
4. Hunter to Wesley, August 29, 1779, in *Early Methodist Preachers*, 2:246.

William Hunter's Story

William Hunter was born near Placey in 1728. He was the son of a farmer, taught to read — particularly Scripture — in addition to learning the trade of farming. He first heard John Wesley preach as a teenager when the famous preacher first travelled to Placey.[5] Wesley's journal dates his first visit to Placey on April 1, 1743, during the revival period of Methodism.[6] Hunter was awakened by Wesley and another Methodist preacher, Mr. Hopper, but his journey toward a devoted Christian life had to overcome harassment from peers and the distractions of adolescence.[7]

The Image of William Hunter from the *Arminian Magazine*.[8]

---

5. Hunter to Wesley, Aug 18, 1779, in *Early Methodist Preachers*, 2:241.

6. "I had a great desire to visit a little village called Placey, about ten measured miles north of Newcastle." Wesley, April 1, 1743, *Journal and Diaries II*, 19: 321. Interestingly, the *Works* editor, Ward, notes that the original journal read "Placey", but the town is actually Plassey. Hunter's account also gives Placey as the town name.

7. Hunter to Wesley, Aug 18, 1779, in *Early Methodist Preachers*, 2:241-242.

8. *Arminian Magazine*, 2 (1779) page not numbered, facing page 589.

Hunter found community among the Methodists with people who offered him companionship, guidance and care.⁹ As well, Hunter found his spiritual home in the Methodist community: he found assurance of forgiveness and he found a place to share this gift with others. He writes, "When I had thus found the goodness of God to my own soul, I could not forbear speaking of it to others."¹⁰ Hunter spread the Christian message in a neighbouring town, where his simple gathering to "talk to them about their souls" was the beginning of a Methodist society.¹¹

During this season of local ministry, Hunter was learning more about the movements of his soul and becoming increasingly aware of the sinfulness in his heart. He longed for a more significant change in his life than had occurred with assurance of pardon. He writes, "but I then read mostly Calvinists' writings, who all write, that sin must be in believers till death: yet I found my mind at times deeply engaged in prayer to be saved from all sin."¹² This reflection shows that in these early days Hunter was discovering the shape of Christian life both through his inner experience and through the teaching of others.

Hunter's exposure to Christian Perfection began when he heard Wesley's sermon on 1 John 1:9: "If we confess our sins, he is faithful and just to forgive us our sins, and to cleanse us from all unrighteousness." (KJV) and it continued when Methodist preacher Mr. Olivers spoke on Perfection by faith in about 1761.¹³ Interestingly, this places Hunter's experiences right around the same time as the Perfectionist controversy was going on in London. Hunter writes,

> About eighteen years ago, it pleased God that I heard Mr. Olivers preach a sermon upon the subject [of Perfection]. His text was, 'Let us go on up to Perfection.' His doctrine was clear, and his arguments strong. My heart consented to the whole truth, and I had clearer views of the way of attaining it, namely, by faith, than ever before. This added new vigour to my spirit, and I seemed to be more on wing than ever. I prayed and wept at his footstool, that He would show me all His salvation. And He gave me to experience such a measure of His grace as I never knew before; a great measure of

---

9. Ibid., 2:242.
10. Ibid., 2:243.
11. Ibid., 2:244.
12. Ibid., 2:247. It should be noted that Calvinists were not the only group that taught that sin would remain in the believer until death; even the Wesleyan Methodists were divided on this point.
13. Hunter to Wesley, in *Early Methodist Preachers*, 2:247-248.

heavenly light and Divine power spread through all my soul; I found disbelief taken away out of my heart; my soul was filled with such faith as I never felt before; my love to Christ was like fire, and I had such views of Him, as my life, my portion, my all, as swallowed me up; and O, how I longed to be with Him! A change passed upon all the powers of my soul, and I felt a great increase of holy and heavenly tempers. I may say, with humility, it was as though I was emptied of all evil, and filled with heaven and God.

Thus, under the influence of His power and grace, I rode upon the sky. My soul fed on angels' food, and I truly ate the bread of heaven. I had more glorious discoveries than ever of the Gospel of God our Saviour, and especially, in His saving the soul from all sin. I enjoyed such an evidence of this in my own mind, as put me beyond all doubt: and yet I never had such a sense of my own littleness, helplessness and unworthiness as now. So true it is, that only grace can humble the soul.[14]

Eighteen years later, when writing his account, Hunter interprets this experience as Christian Perfection. He also states that from that time he became an advocate for the doctrine of Perfection.[15] The narrative letter, as a single snapshot of Hunter's experience, testifies to the lasting effect of the experience. Yet I can imagine there would have also been struggles in his spiritual life that occurred between the transformative experience and his written account.

Furthermore, the two letters continue to tell Hunter's story after his Perfection narrative. His local ministry expanded; he even occasionally offered an exhortation when a preacher failed to come. Hunter's gifts were noticed and he was called by the Methodist conference of preachers into itinerant preaching ministry in 1767.[16] He lived the life of an itinerant preacher in various areas until his death in 1797. Thomas Dodd records Hunter's faithful death in a narrative of Hunter's final weeks.[17] Hunter's last days are filled with praise for God's goodness and Dodd affirms that Hunter died faithfully reflecting the character of a believer who was transformed by an experience of Christian Perfection.[18]

---

14. Ibid., 2:248-249.
15. Ibid., 2:249.
16. Ibid., 2:244.
17. Thomas Dodd to Mr. Mather, Alston-Moor, September 6, 1797, in *Early Methodist Preachers*, 2:251-256.
18. Ibid., 2:256.

William Hunter's Transmission of Christian Perfection through Narrative

William Hunter's spiritual narrative is an example of how the life story of a Methodist was used in the movement to transmit the doctrine of Christian Perfection. In the letters to John Wesley, William Hunter prefaces his spiritual account with his motivation for writing. This account is not a spiritual journal kept to record and evoke spiritual development at the time of the experiences, but rather, a single telling of his life, reflecting backward over time. He writes to John Wesley, "According to your desire, I take the opportunity to write a little of the dealings of God with me; but, as I have not kept any account in writing, many things have slipped my mind."[19] The historical context of this letter is seen through the publication of the letter in the *Arminian Magazine*: John Wesley solicited this account from Hunter. Wesley was in the habit of collecting spiritual accounts for use in encouraging the Methodist communities, first through the practice of letter days, and later in the *Arminian Magazine*.[20] The above letter confirms that William Hunter's account was solicited, maybe even specifically for the *Arminian Magazine*. The two letters appeared in print in November 1779 with the letters dated August 18th and 29th of that same year.[21] With Wesley's knowledge of his preachers, I can imagine that this was not the first time Wesley heard Hunter's narrative. Likely, Wesley saw the potential power of Hunter's story to inspire others. These plausible reasons for soliciting the story suggest how narrative functioned to transmit doctrine throughout the Methodist communities. Through the publication of Hunter's account of his experience, the genre of narrative was used to spread the idea of Christian Perfection.

In addition to the power of narrative used in publication, William Hunter's story also witnesses to the person-to-person spread of the doctrine of Perfection as Hunter both received the doctrine and then passed it along using the medium of preaching. The story began as Hunter heard John Wesley preach in Newcastle on 1 John 1:9: "If we confess our sins, God is faithful and just to forgive us our sins, and to cleanse us from all unrighteousness."[22] Hunter states that he "was clearly convinced of the doctrine of sanctification, and the attainableness of it."[23] Hunter describes the effect the sermon had on him:

---

19. Hunter to Wesley, in *Early Methodist Preachers*, 2:240.
20. For more on letter days and the *Arminian Magazine*, see chapter 5, page 42-43.
21. Ibid., 2:240, 245. Hunter to Wesley, in *Arminian Magazine*, 2:589-598.
22. KJV. Hunter to Wesley, in *Early Methodist Preachers*, 2:247.
23. Ibid.

> I came home with full purpose of heart, not to rest till I was made a living witness of it. I had now a clear view, 1. Of the holiness of God; 2. I had a clear view of the purity and perfection of His law, which is a transcript of the Divine nature. And 3. I felt my great unlikeness to both: and although I felt no condemnation, yet, in the view of these things, I felt much pain in my spirit, and my soul was humbled in the dust before Him! O, how I longed to be made like Him; to love Him with all my heart, soul, mind, and strength![24]

Hunter had received the theology of Perfection from John Wesley and intellectually consented to the idea. But more importantly than intellectual consent, Hunter sensed his own unholiness and the presence of inbred sin in his life which motivated him to seek holiness. Thus the transmission of the doctrine of Christian Perfection through Wesley's preaching inspired Hunter to seek holiness in his own life.

He was taught further about Perfection when he heard Mr. Olivers preach. The content of Olivers' preaching caused another intellectual shift: Hunter now realized that Christian Perfection was to be received by faith. This transmission of doctrine regarding Perfection and faith moved Hunter forward in his search for holiness, which he previously noted was hampered by a lack of faith. He writes, "Sometimes I seemed to be upon the threshold, just stepping into glorious liberty; but again fear and unbelief prevailed, and I started back."[25] Thus, it is in faith that Hunter responded to Olivers' preaching by entering into prayer and after which his narrative of Perfection, quoted above, immediately follows.[26]

The experience of Christian Perfection transformed Hunter's life. He writes in this letter regarding the eighteen years that passed since the time of his experience:

> From the time the Lord gave me to experience this grace, I became an advocate for the glorious doctrine of Christian Perfection: according to the gift He has been pleased to give me, I bear a testimony of it wherever I go; and I never find my soul so happy as when I preach most upon the blessed subject.[27]

---

24. Ibid., 2:247-248.
25. Ibid., 2:248.
26. Ibid., 2:248-249.
27. Ibid.

Fittingly, following the above declaration, in the last few paragraphs of the letter, Hunter illustrates his propensity to preach on Perfection as he gives an explanation of the doctrine.[28] Hunter's narrative of Perfection includes his transformation into a preacher of the doctrine, a preacher who had the witness of his own transformed life as evidence to support his exhortation for others to seek holiness.

Through preaching, Hunter transmitted the doctrine of Perfection, passing along what he had received. The sermonic tone of the conclusion of his letter, noted above, is one example of his exhortation of holiness. The compiler of *The Lives of Early Methodist Preachers* included another example when he supplemented Hunter's narrative letters with additional letters. One letter is from a friend of Hunter's who both honoured Hunter after his death and reproduced a sermon from a set of notes. First, the letter honours Hunter's faithful death (which had occurred only a few months previously) by testifying to his character and to his ministry. His character was holy, characterized by humility, encouragement and care of others.[29] Moreover, his ministry included preaching both repentance and holiness.[30] Second, the letter transcribed from a set of notes a sermon preached by Hunter on Hebrews 6:1 on the topic of Christian holiness.[31]

This letter from Hunter's friend (only identified as F. P.) demonstrates the transmission of the doctrine of Perfection through the life and ministry of Hunter to those to whom he preached. F. P. reports that he was ministered to by Hunter in York during 1773 and 1774. Furthermore, the sermon notes from F. P. confirm Hunter's own claim that he preached Perfection to those in his care. Hunter passed along the doctrine that was preached to him because the experience was so effectual in transforming his life. The doctrinal content of the sermon and the witness to Hunter's holy life (both of which F. P. gave testimony to in his letter) were paired together. This shows how the power of Perfection transformed one life and then through that life the doctrine of Perfection was spread to others in the Methodist communities.

---

28. Ibid., 2:49-250.

29. F. P. to unknown recipient, October 6, 1797, in *Early Methodist Preachers*, 2:258-259.

30. Ibid., 2:257-258.

31. "In looking over some of my papers, I found the following remarks from a sermon of Mr. Hunter's preached in the year 1781, on Christian holiness. Whether I had committed them to writing at the time I heard him preach, or procured them from some friend, I cannot now recollect; but I beg leave to transcribe them, hoping they may be useful to those who are desirous of obtaining purity of heart." Ibid., 2:259. Hebrews 6:1: "Therefore leaving the principles of the doctrine of Christ, let us go on unto perfection" (KJV).

William Hunter Preaching Christian Perfection

William Hunter's narrative shows how when the doctrine of Christian Perfection is embodied, the experience empowers one for ministry. Hunter's narrative illustrates his journey to faith and into ministry. The narrative arc of Hunter's first letter to Wesley recounts his awakening and receiving assurance of pardon. In light of that assurance he stepped into local ministry and then answered the call from the Methodist conference of preachers to begin itinerant preaching. Hunter's story in this first letter to Wesley placed the narrative climax as entrance into ministry in the Methodist connection.[32] But the second letter (written eleven days later) fills out the story that Hunter deemed incomplete. He confesses, "I writ it in haste, I believe it is very imperfect."[33] The second letter recounts Hunter's "being saved from inbred sin," that is, his experience of Christian Perfection.[34] Based on his recollection that the encounter with God happened about eighteen years previous, that would place Hunter's Perfection narrative roughly in the year 1761. That would be during the time of his local ministry, and about six years prior to the beginning of Hunter's time as an itinerant preacher. This also places the experience in the maturing phase of Methodism and in the same time period that the Perfectionist controversy was taking place in London.

Hunter expressed in his letter to Wesley that his Perfection narrative was an important part of his spiritual account. One way that Hunter's Perfection narrative illuminates his account is to show the transformation in his life. This transformation can be seen in three elements of Hunter's account. First, Hunter described his struggle with inbred sin before the experience, as he was awaiting transformation. Second, he used transformative language to describe the experience of Christian Perfection. Finally, Hunter expressed ways in which he was changed by the experience.

First, his description of struggle with sin shows how Hunter's experience of Christian Perfection empowered him to preach by freeing him from the inbred sin and temptation. Hunter tells how God dealt with his soul to make him aware of his great need. He writes,

> I began to be exercised with many uncommon temptations, and felt my own heart ready to comply with the same: this brought me into great straights, and I began to call in question the work of grace in

---

32. Hunter to Wesley, in *Early Methodist Preachers*, 2:240-245.
33. Ibid., 2:245.
34. Ibid., 2:246.

my soul. O, the pain and anguish I felt for weeks together! ... Under this exercise I learned several things. As, first, that my nature was not so much changed as I thought ... I found my mind at times deeply engaged in prayer to be saved from all sin.[35]

Hunter, though already pardoned from sin, was feeling the impact of temptation in his life. Thus, it is clear that his spiritual state before his experience of Christian Perfection was one of struggle. He was longing for freedom and expecting further spiritual transformation.

Second, the language Hunter uses to describe his Perfection experience is poetic imagery that communicates the powerful, direct encounter he had with God. The evocative language illustrates how transforming the experience was in his life. Hunter describes the encounter with God:

a great measure of heavenly light and Divine power spread through all my soul ... I had such views of Him, as my life, my portion, my all as swallowed me up; and O how I longed to be with Him! ... I was emptied of all evil, and filled with heaven and God ... My soul fed on angels' food, and I truly ate the bread of heaven.[36]

Hunter described his encounter with God using language that communicates union with God which is both metaphorical and evocative. Hunter makes the experience appealing to the reader since the encounter significantly affected him. Furthermore, interspersed between the above comments are descriptions of the change this encounter provoked. He writes,

I found unbelief taken away out of my heart; my soul was filled with such faith as I never felt before ... a change passed upon all the powers of my soul, and I felt a great increase of holy and heavenly tempers ... I had more glorious discoveries than ever of the Gospel of God our Saviour, and especially in His saving the soul from all sin. I enjoyed such an evidence of this in my own mind, as put me beyond all doubt.[37]

Hunter describes his Perfection narrative using the language of change. Since this narrative comes years after the experience, I can imagine that this change

---

35. Ibid., 2:246-247.
36. Ibid., 2:248-249.
37. Ibid.

was not only initiated with the experience but also had significant lasting influence deemed relevant when the narrative was told eighteen years later.

The lasting change of a Perfection experience was not guaranteed in Methodist communities.[38] Yet, there is evidence of Hunter's transformed character which is found in the testimony of friends. Thomas Dodd wrote Hunter's faithful death narrative and Hunter's friend, F. P., remarks on both Hunter's character and his faithful ministry over the years. For example, Dodd describes Hunter when it becomes obvious that Hunter is dying: "I was greatly affected with his humble, quiet, composed confidence in God. The preacher and the Christian shone with peculiar lustre: it was evident that he possessed what he had long been with holy fervour inculcating upon others."[39] Dodd observes two things about Hunter in this passage: that he was holy in character, and that he exhorted others to the same. These impressions are witness that Hunter was devoted to preaching the doctrine that impacted his own life. It is worth noting that the genre of the faithful death account does dictate that praise be offered about the faithfulness of the recently deceased. The testimony to a holy character may be unbalanced, as it is lacking an account of any inevitable human failings, but the account need not be taken as fictitious.

Furthermore, Dodd's account of Hunter's final weeks witness to his continued ministry to those around him, even at the age of 69 and in poor health.[40] Hunter was a comfort to those who visited him in his last days. Dodd writes, "When any person came to see him, he was very particular in recommending to them the service of God, with all its attendant comforts; nor did he suffer any to depart without pouring out this solemn benediction upon them."[41] In these final days, Hunter was still embodying faithful ministry to those within his influence. This is evidence of a life lived in ministry, particularly ministry which is empowered by God in response to a transformed life. Indeed, as Hunter neared death Dodd recalls,

> When I entered the room I asked, if he knew me. He whispered, "Yes." I said, "Is God present with you?" he replied three times, "O

---

38. For example, John Wesley notes his disappointment that so many people who claimed an experience of Perfection had lost the benefit of that experience. See John Wesley to Miss March, Bristol, October 13, 1765, in *Letters*, 4:313.

39. Thomas Dodd to unknown recipient, Alston-Moor, September 6, 1797, in *Early Methodist Preachers*, 2:251.

40. As the narrative of Hunter's faithful death begins, Hunter had been caring for the society at Nenthead in Dodd's absence where Hunter preached his final sermon there on July 29, 1797. Ibid., 2:251.

41. Ibid., 2:253.

yes." Upon wetting his lips, he said, "Glory be to God! We should praise Him for everything."[42]

The presence of God marks Hunter's faithful death just as it marked Hunter's Perfection narrative. While this does not prove a consistent experience of the direct presence of God during the interim years, the goal to persevere to faithful death was accomplished.

In addition, there is further witness to Hunter's empowered ministry found in John Wesley's journal and collected letters. Hunter is found in an account relayed by Wesley in his journal among those doing good work and promoting Christian Perfection:

> The rise of the late work was this. William Hunter and John Watson, men not of large gifts, but zealous for Christian perfection, by their warm conversation on the head kindled a flame in some of the leaders. These pressed others to seek after it and for this end appointed meetings for prayer. The fire spread wider and wider till the whole society was in a flame.[43]

Hunter is characterized here as above all else, "zealous for Christian perfection" and the account describes how that zealousness was translated into ministry. As further witness, in the same testimony Hunter is reported to be meeting with those seeking Perfection.[44] Although Hunter's gift of preaching is assessed to be less than outstanding, it is reported in the above quote that Hunter is spreading the doctrine of Perfection in his ministry.[45]

There is further evidence of Hunter's transformation into a preacher as Hunter's friend, F. P., offers a window into Hunter's preaching ministry. As noted above, there are sermon notes recorded by F. P. which summarize a sermon by Hunter exhorting believers on to Perfection. In the sermon Hunter

---

42. Ibid., 2:255.

43. Wesley, June 5, 1772, *Journals and Diaries V*, eds. Ward, Heitzenrater (Nashville: Abingdon, 1993), 22:335. The same account is found as part of the "Short History of the People Called Methodists." John Wesley, *The Methodist Societies*, ed. Davies, vol. 9 of *Works* 9:496.

44. Wesley, June 5, 1772, *Journals and Diaries V*, 22:333. See also *Works*, 9.497.

45. A letter from Wesley a few years later confirms his mild assessment of Hunter's gifts as a preacher: "It was not two or three or a few inconsiderable people who desired that Billy Hunter might stay another year at York, but the stewards and the leaders and the most considerable persons both in respect of grace and understanding. I was agreeably surprised by the account they gave of him, as I had conceived him to be not the best, though not the worst, of our preachers." John Wesley to Christopher Hopper, Rotherham, July 25, 1774, in *Letters*, 6:103.

reminds the listeners to keep their eyes on Christ, and then offers a compelling description of sanctification:

> Sin grows weaker and weaker; Divine love spreads through the soul. Faith grows; and the love of God and man increases. In this temper of mind the believer pants after the full enjoyment of God, and earnestly prays for the accomplishment of His great and precious promises ... When we enter into this great and glorious liberty, the Lord enlarges our capacity, and enables us to make swifter progress in the Divine life. There is a gradual work carried on in the soul after the evils are destroyed, so that we may say to all believers, 'Grow in grace; and go on to higher degrees of evangelical purity.' We receive no new gift, but larger measures of the same love and grace.[46]

Hunter describes in this sermon the desirable season of the spiritual life when love is increasing and God's presence is known intimately. This sermon was preached (according to the notes F. P. cites) in 1781. This would have been about twenty years after his experience of Christian Perfection, and a few years after the autobiographical letters were written to John Wesley. This shows the lasting impact of Hunter's own experience of Christian Perfection. Additionally, Hunter insisted that seeking sanctification is for every believer. Those who had experienced Christian Perfection could be equally seeking holiness and further growth in grace, as those who had yet to experience Perfection.

Hunter embodies Christian Perfection illustrating how the experience of Perfection empowers the believer for ministry. Hunter communicated the doctrine of Christian Perfection through preaching. Furthermore, his Perfection narrative and his holy life after his experience both witness, along with his words, to how Christian Perfection empowers the believer.

The narrative of William Hunter, farmer by birth but Methodist lay preacher by calling, is a witness of the power of Christian Perfection to both transform a life and empower ministry which transmits the idea of Perfection to others. Hunter received teaching on Perfection through the preaching of Wesley and Olivers and he experienced a direct encounter with God that transformed his life. The transformation was expressed, in part, through preaching the doctrine that was so powerful in his own life. William Hunter

---

46. F. P., in *Early Methodist Preachers*, 2:259-260.

offers an embodied witness to the transmission of Christian Perfection through the pairing of a holy life and preaching the doctrine.

9

Bathsheba Hall and Growth in Grace

> I feel a holy, solid peace, though with great weakness of body, and much lowness of spirits. Indeed my whole frame is exceedingly disordered: but, glory be to God, I rest in his Will. I have no will either for life or death. All is well; for Christ is mine.
>
> Bathsheba Hall, April 23, 1771[1]

Introducing the excerpts from the journal of Mrs. Bathsheba Hall's (1745–1780), which was published in the *Arminian Magazine* in 1781, John Wesley commends her journal as "the genuine picture of a soul renewed in love, and wholly devoted to God."[2] Three months previously Wesley commented in his journal that he had preached the funeral sermon for "that blessed saint, Bathsheba Hall."[3] This esteem from Wesley speaks to the character of a woman who was spiritually influential during her lifetime. Bathsheba Hall worked in her local community of Bristol to draw nearer to God, and to draw others to God with her. Yet, along with this simplicity comes the extraordinary experience of encountering God in an experience of Christian Perfection. Hall's humble testimony to her experience offered inspiration and example to other Methodists. In addition, her story enlightens us about both the power of testimony for the transmission of Christian Perfection, and sheds light on the daily ebb and flow of spirituality after an experience of Perfection.

Bathsheba Hall's life is seen through her journal excerpted in the *Arminian Magazine* from January through July in 1781, beginning only a few months after her death.[4] Additionally, John Wesley mentions Hall and her husband in

---

1. Bathsheba Hall, "An Extract from the Diary of Mrs. Bathsheba Hall," in *Arminian Magazine*, 4 (1781) 150.

2. Ibid., 4:35.

3. Wesley, October, 1, 1780, *Journal and Diaries VI*, in *Works*, 23:187.

4. Hall, *Arminian Magazine*, 4:35–40, 94–97, 148–152, 195–198, 256–259, 309–311, 372–376.

his journal as local saints while passing through Bristol in September 1779.[5] The above note that Wesley preached Hall's funeral sermon is the only other mention in Wesley's journal. The impact of her life was local, but spiritually significant for those to whom she ministered.

Bathsheba Hall's Story

Bathsheba Hall was born in December 1745 in the Bristol area. She went to London as a young woman where she had a conversion experience in 1763 at the age of seventeen, near the height of the Perfectionist controversy. Her conversion took place while she was among the Methodists and living in John Wesley's house.[6] Wesley notes in his introduction to the journal that she married John Hall, although her journal does not mention her husband in the published extracts.[7] Sometime after her marriage, Hall returned to Bristol. In his journal John Wesley notes that the Methodist community in Bristol had significant spiritual gains after the Halls arrived there.[8]

The published journal excerpts begin with an extended narrative of Hall's Perfection experience. The narrative includes a brief preamble about her conversion,[9] but the narrative arc begins with her encounter with a woman who claimed "the Great Salvation," or Christian Perfection.[10] This encounter awakened in Hall the desire for a deeper experience of God in addition to her conversion experience.

Similar to other Perfection narratives, Hall's account shows that longing after and seeking Perfection came with an increased awareness of her own sinfulness. She observes that she was drawing near to God even with the increasing awareness of her sin and suffering. She writes,

> The more I approached the Lord in secret, the more was the mystery of iniquity discovered. At the same time the Lord permitted me to be tried with a variety of outward things: but these were nothing to what I suffered within. O who can describe this state of insensibility? When the soul can neither read nor pray, neither wrestle nor strive,

---

5. Wesley, Sept 23, 1779, *Journal and Diaries VI*, *Works*, 23:149.

6. Hall, *Arminian Magazine*, 4:35. Her exact birthdate is either Dec 12 or 27. She celebrates her twentieth birthday on December 12, and her twenty-seventh on December 27, idem., 4:35, 374.

7. Hall, *Arminian Magazine*, 4:35.

8. Wesley, Sept 23, 1779, *Journal and Diaries VI*, *Works*, 23:149.

9. Hall, *Arminian Magazine*, 4:35.

10. Ibid., 4:36.

but only hang naked upon God? For some weeks I was in this insensible state. And from that hour my will was entirely subject to the will of God: yet he shewed me, I had more battles to fight, that my soul was not yet all-renewed.[11]

Hall astutely observes how after conversion God continued to work to sanctify her life.

Hall goes on to narrate an ecstatic experience of God that is consistent with the Perfection narratives of other Methodists, even though she does not use the term Christian Perfection:

About the middle of January, 1769, as I was with my dear friend, *Ann B—*, before the Lord, my mind was in a violent motion, such as it is not possible to express. It was as if my soul and body were separated with these words, *I will: Be Thou Clean*. But still there was a fear of being deceived; till as soon as I rose on Sunday morning, I heard the voice of my Beloved saying, *Thou art all fair: there is no spot in thee*. I then felt nothing rapturous, but a holy joy and solid peace such as I expect to feel in Glory.[12]

Hall continues the narrative as she seeks the assurance that the experience is genuine through prayer with another friend. She writes,

As soon as we bowed before the Lord, our first petition was, *Let there be light in our dwellings*. In that moment the Lord came as a mighty rushing wind, which filled all the room. So great was the glory of the Lord, we could not utter a word. Immediately I felt that I was sealed with the holy Spirit of Promise.[13]

Hall's Perfection narrative chronicles several months, from the time when she began to seek the Great Salvation at the end of 1767 until the ecstatic encounters with God in January of 1769 which she relates here. This extended narrative is at the beginning of the journal extracts that John Wesley published. Hall's story has just begun when she tells her Perfection account.

The rest of the journal extracts published in the *Arminian Magazine* mainly chronicle Hall's spiritual life, but some biographical details are also revealed.

---

11. Ibid., 4:37.
12. Ibid., 4:38. Emphasis in original.
13. Ibid., 4:39.

It seems that Bathsheba Hall lived with serious chronic illness which included significant physical pain.[14] Death was often near because of her illness, but it only drew her closer to God and caused her to hope for the joys of heaven.[15]

She notes that she was hindered from going to public worship (probably by illness), yet this does not hinder her celebration of the Sabbath and her communion with God.[16] On the contrary, her ministry of intercessory prayer for the salvation and Perfection of others was not hindered by her physical limitations; it might have even been enhanced because her physical limitations allowed more time for prayer.[17] Likewise, her physical suffering did not cause doubt about God's presence or His care for her. As seen in the epigraph, she writes,

> Thursday [April] 23 [1771]. I feel a holy, solid peace, though with great weakness of body, and much lowness of spirits. Indeed my whole frame is exceedingly disordered: but, glory be to God, I rest in his Will. I have no will either for life or death. All is well; for Christ is mine.[18]

In this entry and throughout Hall's journal she articulates that spiritual well being is a gift from God in the midst of physical suffering.

Hall's ministry in Bristol, chronicled in the journal excerpts, was personal and local. She prayed with individuals, particularly to be freed from inbred sin and receive greater salvation.[19] Moreover, her ministry extended outside of Bristol to friends in the nearby town of Bath in the mode of letters and visits.[20]

The published journal excerpts focus on 1771-1772, a few years in her mid-twenties. During this time as Hall continued to grow in grace after her Perfection experience; she revelled in the continued blessing of freedom from her enemies — a metaphor she used for the inbred sin that plagued her.[21] The final journal entry included in the *Arminian Magazine* is from 1775, five years

---

14. For example, see the journal entry for March 4, 1771, Ibid., 4:40. See also 4:97, 150, 152, 195, 196, 309, 310.

15. Ibid., 4:36, 256, 257, 258, 375.

16. Ibid., 4:95, 257.

17. Ibid., 4:95.

18. Ibid., 4:150.

19. Ibid., 4:94-95. "I was sensible this night, of the great importance of wrestling with God for the souls of others. O what a great thing it is, to be all on the Lord's side!" Idem., 4:94-95. See also the entry for May 2, 1772, idem., 4:310.

20. Ibid., 4:96, 196, 258.

21. Ibid., 4:37, 311.

before her death.[22] In September, 1780 she died at the age of 34 and John Wesley notes in his journal: "about two, I preached a funeral sermon at Kingswood for that blessed saint, Bathsheba Hall, a pattern for many years of zealously doing and patiently suffering the will of God."[23] Hall's short life of growth in grace is a witness to the embodiment of the doctrine of Christian Perfection.

Bathsheba Hall's Transmission of Christian Perfection through Narrative

Bathsheba Hall is the most striking example among the case studies in this thesis of how small scale, personal ministry of sharing her narrative caused the idea and experience of Perfection to spread through Britain in Methodist circles. Three different levels of the power of narrative can be seen in Hall's journal. First, she was encouraged toward Perfection through the personal narrative of a fellow believer. Second, she encountered God and was perfected in love while sharing her struggle and story with friends. Finally, multiple times her humble expressions of her own "Experience" not only inspired the pursuit of holiness but immediately evoked for another believer an ecstatic encounter with God.

To begin, Hall received the doctrine of Perfection through the narrative of others. The story of Perfection began when Hall first heard about Perfection about a year after her conversion, but the idea had little effect on her at that time. Later she heard about the doctrine of Perfection (called the Great Salvation in this instance) through a personal encounter. She writes,

> In the latter end of the year 1767 [four years after her conversion], God sent one of his dear people to see me, who had been long a witness of the Great Salvation. May that sacred day never be forgotten! She gave me a clear and full account of what she experienced. God applied it strongly to my heart, and beamed forth on my soul in a wonderful manner.[24]

The encounter with this woman who shared her own narrative and the testimony of the holiness of life impacted Hall's life dramatically. The focus of the rest of the journal is Hall's pursuit of holiness.

The next stage in Hall's journey as she experiences Christian Perfection intertwines narrative and community. Two friends played a role in Hall's

---

22. Ibid., 4:374.
23. Wesley, October 1, 1780, *Journal and Diaries VI, Works*, 23:187.
24. Hall, *Arminian Magazine*, 4:36.

Perfection experience: one she calls "Ann B—", the other "Eliz. T." In her narrative Hall recounts Ann's presence during her Perfection experience:

> About the middle of January, 1769, as I was with my dear friend, Ann B—, before the Lord, my mind was in a violent motion, such as it is not possible to express. It was as if my soul and body were separated with these words, *I will: Be thou clean*. But still there was a fear of being deceived.[25]

Together these two women shared their struggle, and together they were seeking after the witness to God's cleansing that John Wesley declared accompanies Christian Perfection.[26] Soon she received it: "I rose on Sunday morning, I heard the voice of my Beloved saying, *Thou art all fair: there is no spot in thee*. I felt nothing rapturous, but a holy joy and solid peace such as I expect to feel in Glory."[27] Hall's immediate response was to share this experience with a friend: "That day, and not before, could I speak of it. I went to my dear friend Eliz. T. and freely told her what the gracious Lord had done for my soul."[28] The encounter with God that Hall experienced was received through sharing her life and struggles with her friend Ann, and immediately was shared with her friend Elizabeth in response to the joy of the encounter. Hall's story is an example of how narrative is embedded in community as she shared her experience with others.

The transmission of the doctrine of Perfection continued as Hall shared her story with her friend. When Elizabeth heard about the experience of Hall, she desired the same and both women responded to Elizabeth's desire for Perfection as they prayed together:

> [Elizabeth] came up on January 30th [1769]; … As soon as we bowed before the Lord, our first petition was, *Let there be light in our dwellings*. In that moment the Lord came as a mighty rushing wind, which filled all the room. So great was the glory of the Lord, we could not utter a word. Immediately I felt that I was sealed with the holy Spirit of Promise. When the mighty power abated, I was permitted to plead with God, as it were face to face, for my friend;

---

25. Ibid., 4:38.
26. For John Wesley's thoughts on the seal of the Spirit, see John Wesley to Thomas Olivers, Lewisham, March 24, 1757, in *Letters*, 3:213.
27. Hall, *Arminian Magazine*, 4:38.
28. Ibid.

and was answered, *The Egyptians whom she hath seen to day, she shall see no more for ever.* At the same time the promise was given to *me*, God applied it to *her* soul.[29]

For Hall and Elizabeth, the sharing of story and sharing the spiritual journey together led to a direct encounter with God.

Later in the journal Hall recounts reading her "Experience" to others whom she encouraged to seek Perfection.[30] It appears that the Perfection narrative found at the beginning of the published journal is the written document Hall refers to as her "Experience." I can also imagine that Hall read this narrative many times when she shared about her transformative encounter with God. Sharing her narrative was a natural way that Hall spread the idea of Christian Perfection as she provided spiritual leadership in Bristol.

In particular, there are two accounts of Hall sharing her Experience recorded in the published journal. The first is from the journal entry for September 18, 1771 and tells the story of M. Stokes:

> Wednesday [September] 18 [1771]. I asked *M. Stokes* to come home with me, and I would read her my Experience. While I was reading, I felt the mighty power of God descend upon me, and my soul overflowed with gratitude to him, who reigned in me without a rival. We then went to prayer, and strong faith was given me, to wrestle for my friend. She cried out in great agony of soul. I prayed on, till she fainted away. When she recovered, she said, "The Lord has done something for me, but I know not what." I said, Wait, and he will answer for himself.[31]

This encounter shows three interesting things about the transmission of the idea and experience of Christian Perfection. First, this vignette is evidence that Hall had a written account of her spiritual experience which she was willing to share with others. The presence of a written narrative of her experience indicates the importance of that particular experience in her own self-understanding. In her journal there are many accounts of how Hall met God, but there was something particular about her experience of Christian Perfection narrated at

---

29. Ibid., 4:38, 39. Emphasis in original.
30. Ibid., 4:197, 373. Hall referred to what she shared as her "Experience" which seems to indicate a particular written account of a spiritual experience.
31. Ibid., 4:197.

the beginning of her journal that sets it apart from other experiences of daily communion with God.

Second, it is interesting that Stokes would visit Hall to hear the experience and to receive prayer. This episode is a glimpse into the spirituality of this Methodist community which included social visits. Discipleship occurred personally one on one, not simply in the organized groups in the Methodist connection.

Finally, Hall humbly waited for God to interpret the experience rather than imposing her own experience on her friend. Hall communicated that if this was an experience of Christian Perfection for Stokes, that God would interpret it and confirm it Himself. Hall felt no pressure herself to define the experience for Stokes.

The second account of sharing her Experience is found about a year later in the journal. This journal entry tells the story of an unnamed woman:

> Thursday [December] 17 [1772]. The Lord sent one of his dear children to me, who found pardon last winter, but was now in deep distress through inbred sin, and longed for deliverance. I read her my own experience. While I was reading, my soul was overwhelmed with the power of God. We went to prayer. She was shook as over the mouth of hell. She cried out, "I am just like Satan. It is not possible, God should save such a wretch as *me*." For some time she continued in a deep agony. We wrestled with God about an hour. God then began to shine upon her soul. I then left her alone: and her light and love gradually increased till we parted. The next day she came again; and while we were pouring out our souls in prayer, the Lord came down as a mighty rushing wind, and filled her soul with himself.[32]

Similar to Hall's encounter with Stokes, this encounter includes Hall's written account of her experience. Again, the act of sharing narrative of her experience evoked an experience of God in the listener. It is hard to tell from this excerpt what exactly was the experience of the listener, perhaps Christian Perfection or perhaps some other encounter with God, as Hall is minimal in her interpretation of her listener's experience.[33] She simply reports her own

---

32. Ibid., 4:373.

33. Although Hall does not explicitly testify that the women she read her Experience to experienced Christian Perfection, she does record when some people to whom she ministered had an experience of Christian Perfection. First, her friend in Bath who had been seeking Perfection received it. See entry for

impression of God's presence as a mighty rushing wind, which relates to another observation about this account. It is striking that this account is filled with metaphorical language to try to express the experience. God is experienced as power, light and wind.

Another notable aspect of this encounter is the ongoing process of discipleship between these two women. Although there is an ecstatic encounter the day Hall read her experience, the woman came back the next day for prayer again. Hall exhibits humility, by accepting that simply reading the experience and praying does not demand a response from God. Her response to her friend's encounter with God was that she continued to pray with her friend for freedom from inbred sin.

The transmission of the idea of Perfection was carried along this chain of discipleship through the sharing of narrative. In mimetic fashion Hall heard someone's experience of Perfection, and then she shared her own. The experience of Perfection enabled her to humbly pass along the blessing to others. Although the encounters with God that Hall's friends had are not designated as Perfection experiences, I can imagine that the impact of hearing about Hall's experience had a similar effect to when Hall heard the Christian Perfection narrative from a fellow Methodist. Furthermore, I can imagine that those who heard Hall's story — Eliz. T., M. Stokes and the unnamed woman — also told their stories to others and the chain of transmission continued. How interesting it would be to find the journal of these women and see how the narrative of Perfection continued to spread.

The experience of Christian Perfection did not remain a private experience for Hall that simply empowered her ministry, but rather, her narrative of Perfection became the content of her ministry to others. These stories of transmission in Bathsheba Hall's journal show that her ability to tell the narrative of the particular event of Christian Perfection shaped her ministry. Furthermore, the journal entries narrate how Hall received and passed along the idea of Christian Perfection.

Bathsheba Hall and Growth in Grace

Bathsheba Hall embodies the doctrine of Christian Perfection by illuminating how, after her initial experience of Perfection, she continued to grow in grace. Bathsheba Hall's story shares the characteristics of a Perfection experience with the other narratives examined in this book. But, more so than

Sept 13, 1771, ibid., 4:196. Also, Hall recounts two men she was connected to receiving the greater salvation, see May 30, 1772, idem., 4:311.

other accounts, Hall's journal after her Perfection narrative illustrates how a Perfected life is one that is growing in the knowledge of God and acting in obedience to His call.

The first journal entry after Hall's Perfection narrative indicates her purpose for writing the journal. On February 28, 1771, Hall writes, "Lord, I begin this Account, by offering it up to thee, with a single eye to thy glory: I believe, thou hast called me thus to recount thy noble acts."[34] She set apart this journal as a place to express the work of God in her life. The next day she added another goal to the journal and to this season in her life: "March 1. I stand in need of much wisdom, to understand the different operations of the Holy Spirit on my soul."[35] This period of her life is marked by self-examination in an attempt to grow in holiness. It is a time of growth in holiness and subsequent journal entries show it is also a season of physical suffering and of a growing ministry to those around her.

Many of the journal entries express Hall's gratitude (or possibly astonishment) that she continues to be blessed with the gift of Christian Perfection and God's presence that accompanied it. For example, on March 21, 1771, more than two years after her Perfection experience she writes, "For two years past, I can truly say I have desired nothing but God. Through the blood of the Lamb, I continually enter into rest. Not unto me, but unto his name be the praise!"[36] Later she writes,

> Tuesday [April] 2 [1771], I felt much of his soul-reviving power. But O! What ignorance remains upon my mind? I feel a thirst for divine knowledge; a contending with the Lord for spiritual wisdom. I am waiting at Wisdom's gate! Speak, Lord; for they servant heareth.[37]

Here Hall's gratitude leads her to seek God for more wisdom.

Similarly, a letter from a friend who is in the season of longing for Perfection evokes thankfulness in Hall:

> I received a letter from *Bath*, from one that is athirst for full salvation. How shall I sufficiently praise God for giving *me* to enjoy and witness that perfect love, which casteth out all fear that hath torment?

---

34. Ibid., 4:39.
35. Ibid.
36. Ibid., 4:96–97.
37. Ibid., 4:149.

I shall fear God, but in a manner I did not once. I come before him with holy boldness, and reverential awe![38]

Hall observes the transformation of her life in response to her experience of Perfection: fear has been transformed into holy boldness and awe. Each of these journal entries show that Hall was continuing to experience the freedom and joy that accompanied her experience of Perfection.

Furthermore, Hall's journal witnesses to her growth in grace by illustrating how after her Perfection experience her awareness of sin did not bring self-condemnation, but rather, it turned her heart to Christ in thankfulness and humility. For example, on March 23, 1771, she writes,

> I adore thee, O thou Fountain of all blessedness, and abhor myself in dust and ashes! O that I could stand every moment on my watch-tower, with my lamp and my light burning!
>
> I know I have spoken many words today that will not bear the Divine scrutiny. But
> "I see the Lamb in glory stands:
> And spreads for me his bleeding hands."[39]

Likewise, on November 5, 1771, she writes,

> Out of the depth of my poverty and vileness do I cry unto thee, O Lord! Surely never was a soul so needy! so divested of joy and comfort! Lord, thou knowest which way to make me conformable to thy death. I yield, O my God! to the painful stroke. All my desire is to be made like unto thee in all things![40]

These entries show that this season of increased peace and communion with God did not exclude times of suffering, both physical and spiritual. Yet, Hall's journal expresses that when she struggled, she turned to God and did not despair. The next entry, on November 7th — just two days after the troubled entry above — she writes,

> My soul was refreshed this day with the multitude of peace. I felt the holy presence of my God and my All: and I had sweet communion

---

38. Ibid., 4:96.
39. Ibid., 4:97.
40. Ibid., 4:257. One of the few editorial insertions is after this entry. The editor, Wesley, adds in brackets: "I doubt not but this pain was partly nervous, and partly diabolical."

> with the saints, though absent in body. How thankful is the soul, after a day of trouble, for the least of these consolations![41]

Through the honesty of her journal, Hall shows the reader that growth in maturity does not remove all awareness of sinfulness. Instead, Hall exhibits an increased ability to turn to God in the midst of struggle.

Another way that Hall was growing in this time was through her devotedness to others. She was not a lay preacher like Crosby or Hunter or the many other preachers in the Methodist connection, but she engaged in local ministry as part of the Methodist structures. Fellowship and acts of mercy were an essential part of spirituality for those who were members of Methodist societies.[42] Hall felt the needs of the world around her when she looked around at the town she lived in. On March 28, 1771 she observes:

> I have been among the people of the world to-day: O my soul, who maketh thee to differ? The Lord, the Lord God, merciful and gracious: may I be forever bowed in deep abasement before him! He has indeed set his mark upon me. I pant for deeper devotedness to him![43]

Likewise, on April 4, 1771 she felt the pain of the world: "Passing through the town to-night, what exquisite pain did I feel! What disorder! What sin of every kind! How does *the whole world lie in the wicked one!*"[44] I can imagine that Hall's concern for the world expressed in these entries evoked a response of action in many forms. One way her concern is expressed in her journal is her care for fellow Methodists. She ministered through letters to those who were in the neighbouring town of Bath.[45] She also ministered through intercessory prayer, which she describes as wrestling with God on behalf of others.[46] Finally, her mere presence and character as a godly woman also was a ministry to those around her. For example:

> Wednesday [April] 3 [1771], Business called me to see one, that *was* serious [about God], but is now deeply revolted. I went with

---

41. Ibid., 4:257.
42. Wesley, "*Directions Given to the Band-Societies*, Dec 25, 1744," in *Methodist Societies*, vol. 9 in *Works*, 79. See also Albin, "Inwardly Persuaded," 50, regarding the dual focus of the select societies.
43. Hall, *Arminian Magazine*, 4:97.
44. Ibid., 4:149. Emphasis in original.
45. Ibid., 4:96, 196, 258.
46. Ibid., 4:94-95. Idem., 4:310.

much prayer. As soon as I entered the room, he seemed struck with a solemn awe. O how solemn should the deportment of a Christian be! that all who see him may take knowledge he has been with Jesus. After I came home, I felt such love as I cannot describe and much power to wrestle with God for him.[47]

This encounter shows how Hall's life after her experience of Perfection was visibly characterized by faithfulness and purity, shown by both the recognition of her godliness by this man, and also by her humble response to engage in prayer for him.

In addition to the evidence in her journal of ways in which she was being shaped by holiness of life and growth in grace, Hall also makes explicit comments about what she perceived was happening in her life after her Perfection experience. Fitting with her expressed goal in the early journal entries, she became self-reflective and began to understand the workings of the Spirit in her soul. For example, she used the language of 2 Peter 1:4 and expressed that a life of holiness is made possible by becoming a partaker in the divine nature. She writes, "The capacity of my soul seems enlarged, my intellectual faculties expanded wider for the Deity. How can we escape the pollutions that are in the world, but by being made partakers of the Divine Nature?"[48] Similarly, three days later Hall expresses her understanding of the presence of God with her:

> Wednesday [October] 24 [1771]. I know that God dwelleth in me, and I in God, by the Spirit that he hath given me. One was saying, "Many look for the rooting out of Sin, but do not look for an indwelling God." But they cannot be divided. If any sin remains, God does not dwell in that heart. But if sin is cast out, then we know that the Lord, the King is in the midst of us.[49]

Hall is self-reflective here as she observes her experience of God's presence which has expelled sin. In addition, she generalized her experience to a doctrine that would apply to others. From this observation and from her prayers for others, it is evident that Hall takes sin seriously as a problem, but also she held out great hope that God can and will remove sin from the life of a believer. This

47. Ibid., 4:149.
48. Ibid., 4:150.
49. Ibid., 4:150-151. Interestingly, she is alluding to Zephaniah 3:15 in her reference to the King being in the midst and she quoted that Scripture in her journal entry mentioned above about seeking self-reflectiveness. See entry for March 1, 1771, idem., 4:39.

confidence was paired with the assurance that God was the one doing the work to sustain the purity of her heart: "Happy am I, that the Lord is the guardian of that pure love which he has breathed into my soul!"[50] Hall recognized that there was continued growth in holiness, even along with her assertion that sin did not remain.

Similarly, Hall recognized that there was much to learn even after her initial Perfection experience. On October 6, 1771 she shows how much more she has to learn and references her Perfection experience by quoting the Scripture words that she heard spoken to her ("I will, be thou clean").[51] She writes,

> I cannot be sufficiently thankful, that God has brought me into the narrow path of holiness. Many talk of devotedness to God; but few experience it. The soul which desires nothing but God, has many deaths to pass through even after the Lord has spoken that word, "I will: be thou clean!" In order to a higher degree of real life, it will be called to die daily. Happy soul, that can say, under every operation of the Spirit, "Not as I will; but as though wilt."[52]

Hall holds in tension that she has had the experience of cleansing at the centre of her Perfection narrative, yet also she does not deny the reality that God will continue to teach her new things and cause her to growth in grace.

Hall's self-reflection, descriptions of her acts of mercy and humble thankfulness for God's gift of grace, illustrate the holy character that was being formed in her life as a result of the freedom that her Perfection experience evoked. The picture of a holy life that emerges from Hall's journal brings the doctrine described by John and Charles Wesley to life as she lived out holiness, notwithstanding the struggles of her daily life.

In conclusion, Bathsheba Hall's journal offers a glimpse into life which continues to grow and mature after the transformative experience of Christian Perfection. She received inspiration from witnesses to Perfection that provoked her spiritual development, and in response shared her blessing by ministering to others. Her journal offers a humble source of early Methodist spiritual reflection, since it was not composed to justify her spiritual leadership nor to argue a theological position, but rather, it was composed as a tool for

---

50. Ibid., 4:197.
51. Ibid., 4:38.
52. Ibid., 4:197.

self-reflection and growth. John Wesley's intended purpose for publishing the journal was accomplished as her journal offers inspiration to others by showing "the genuine picture of a soul renewed in love, and wholly devoted to God."[53] The journal of Bathsheba Hall offers an embodied picture of Christian Perfection that humanizes the image of the perfect Christian, making the ideal more complex by including suffering and struggles along with success. The very ordinariness of her life was touched with the extraordinary gift of Christian Perfection. Because of all this, Hall's story enriches the understanding of the early Methodist doctrine of Christian Perfection.

---

53. Wesley, *Arminian Magazine*, 4:35.

10

The Elements of Perfection Narratives

From the study of Perfection narratives some conclusions about these early Methodist narratives can be made. The stories in this book are indeed narratives. They were written and published making use of the genre of narrative in the medium of letters and journals, and published in magazines and collections of lives. Aristotle's classic narrative theory from his work on poetics frames the following conclusions. Aristotle states that stories have a beginning, middle and end.[1]

First, in the beginning, most of the stories express the spiritual state of the person after conversion: they are distraught by an increasing awareness of sin. Next, in the middle, there is gradual growth in grace marked at the climax with a direct experience of God. In the end, the narrative after a Perfection experience shows that the author is transformed, yet continues growing in grace.

Beginning – Sin in the Believer

The beginning of the Perfection narrative establishes tension in the life of the subject when sin is found to be present even after conversion and assurance of pardon. The narratives of Perfection often include the conversion of the person, as a sort of preamble, but the real narrative tension is established in their search for holiness. This search is undertaken alongside the discovery of sin that remains even after assurance of pardon. The discovery of this sin, described by John Wesley as inbred sin, creates some anxiety, not unlike the sorrow for sin described in Christian tradition as compunction. Yet, the discovery of sin also moves the narrative forward as the subject seeks holiness in deeper ways.[2]

---

1. Aristotle established that a key element to story is wholeness marked by an intentional beginning, middle and end. Aristotle, *Poetics*, ed. and trans. Stephen Halliwell, Loeb Classical Library (Cambridge, MA: Harvard University Press, 1995), 55.

For example, the experience of the unnamed man narrated in his letter to John Wesley and examined in chapter five illustrates the experience of discovering sin after justification. He writes, "for some time I lived in a clear sense of pardon: but I saw by degrees such a depth of wickedness in my heart, that I have many times wondered how I stood under it, without giving up all for lost."[3] It was a significant part of this man's journey toward Perfection to become aware of his deeper need for Christ that existed beyond pardon of sin.

Recognizing sin after conversion sets the stage for receiving grace from God. In his sermon "The Repentance of Believers," John Wesley argues that both repentance and faith are the proper response to this discovery of sin. He writes,

> Thus it is that in the children of God repentance and faith exactly answer each other. By repentance we feel the sin remaining in our hearts, and cleaving to our words and actions. By faith we receive the power of God in Christ, purifying our hearts and cleansing our hands.... Repentance says, 'Without him I can do nothing:' faith says, 'I can do all things through Christ strengthening me.' Through him I cannot only overcome, but expel all the enemies of my soul. Through him I can 'love the Lord my God with all my heart, mind, soul, and strength;' yea, and walk in holiness and righteousness before him all the days of my life.[4]

The pairing of faith with the discovery of inbred sin provides hope for a way forward, instead of falling into despair of never being rid of sin. Christian Perfection is received by faith, the topic of the middle of the narratives.

Middle – Perfection by Faith & a Direct Encounter with God

The middle of the narrative of Perfection explores sanctification in the life of the subject, both in slow gradual growth and in an instantaneous experience. The middle of the narrative is the most substantial in the life of the believer. Two aspects of the instantaneous experience are common in many of the narratives: that Perfection is received by faith and that the instantaneous experience is marked by a direct encounter with God.

---

2. For examples, see Hall, *Arminian Magazine*, 4:36. Clark, *Arminian Magazine*, 5:351. Letter from an unnamed man to Wesley, *Arminian Magazine*, 4:162.

3. An unnamed man to Wesley, in *Arminian Magazine*, 4:162.

4. Wesley, Sermon 14, "Repentance", § II.6 in *Works*, 1:349-350.

To begin, Perfection received by faith is illustrated by Sarah Crosby. In her 1773 letter to John Wesley, she describes that her struggle toward Perfection was hampered by her lack of faith, as she was seeking Perfection through increased self-knowledge rather than by faith. She writes,

> my Lord instructed me as a little child, daily showing me how wrong my former judgement [regarding the importance of self-knowledge] had been, from feeling myself still surrounded with various infirmities and yet a sweet, constant union with him, which these [infirmities] did not interrupt nor would they have interrupted before but through want of faith. So that I now saw every failure in obedience was for want of more faith.[5]

For Crosby, the Perfection that came from union with Christ was made possible through faith. In addition, obedience was made possible by faith and knowing God, not by knowing the depth of sin more thoroughly.

Furthermore, John Wesley argues for receiving sanctification by faith as he contrasts it with receiving sanctification by works:

> Certainly you may look for [sanctification] *now*, if you believe it is by faith. And by this token you may surely know whether you seek it by faith or by works. If by works, you want something to be done *first*, before you are sanctified. You think, I must first *be* or *do* thus or thus. Then you are seeking it by works unto this day. If you seek it by faith, you may expect it as *you are*; and expect it *now*.[6]

Sanctification by faith, as invoked by John Wesley above, makes possible the assertion that Christian Perfection is both a gradual growth and an instantaneous event. By faith it is received over a season of faithfully seeking God. Likewise, by faith it is received in a moment because sanctification is the work of God, to do when He pleases. When received by faith, the believer can attribute the sanctifying work to God, just as William Hunter does in his letter of testimony: "Glory be to His name, I find my soul united to Him."[7]

---

5. Crosby to Wesley, in *Early Methodist Spirituality*, 266.

6. John Wesley, Sermon 43, "The Scripture Way of Salvation" §III.18 in *Sermons II: 34-70*, ed. Albert C. Outler, vol. 2 of *The Bicentennial Edition of The Works of John Wesley*, ed. Frank Baker (Nashville: Abingdon Press, 1985), 2:169.

7. Hunter to Wesley, *Early Methodist Preachers*, 2:249.

In addition to Perfection by faith, John Wesley described sanctification both as growing gradually and as coming instantaneously, with the instantaneous event of Christian Perfection acting as the centre of narratives of Perfection. In spiritual letters this instantaneous event appears as a narrative climax.[8] As seen in chapter eight, for William Hunter, the event warrants a second letter to transmit his spiritual account faithfully.[9] Similarly, in both the journals of Bathsheba Hall and George Clark an entry containing an extended narrative of the instantaneous event interrupts shorter entries, and in these journals the date of this event is remembered on anniversaries of the experience.[10] Furthermore, there are aspects of the narrative that mark this particular encounter with God as out of the ordinary, such as that the subject encountered God in a particularly intimate way: seeing visions, or hearing promises — usually in the words of Scripture. Additionally, the event is experienced in bodily ways with tears, trembling, and even fainting.[11]

Looking more carefully at this instantaneous event, many Methodists received words of Scripture, as if spoken to them, during their experience of Perfection. The words of Scripture were experienced as personalized to speak to the concern or worry that held them back from trusting in God.[12] For example, Bathsheba Hall received words of Scripture twice during her Perfection narrative. She writes,

> It was as if my soul and body were separated with these words, *I will: Be thou clean* [Jesus heals a leper: parallel passages in Matthew 8:3; Mark 1:41: Luke 5:13]. But still there was a fear of being deceived; till as soon as I rose on Sunday morning, I heard the voice of my

---

8. For examples, see the following letters in the *Arminian Magazine*: An unnamed man to Wesley, in *Arminian Magazine*, 4:162-165. Mrs. E. M—n to Wesley, in *Arminian Magazine*, 4:444-445. Miss JCM to John Wesley, October 7, 1762, in *Arminian Magazine*, 5:327-329.

9. Hunter to Wesley, *Early Methodist Preachers*, 2:245-246. See chapter eight, page 88.

10. The Perfection narrative of George Clark dominates the twelfth journal excerpt: see Clark, *Arminian Magazine*, 6:244-246. Also, Clark marks the one year anniversary, and reflects back after two years and one month. Clark, *Arminian Magazine*, 6:301, 6:354. Also, Bathsheba Hall reflects back after two years. Hall, *Arminian Magazine*, 4:96-97.

11. For example, Clark experienced tears and trembling, Clark, *Arminian Magazine*, 6:246. Bathsheba Hall's friend, M. Stokes, fainted. Hall, *Arminian Magazine*, 4:197.

12. Similarly, Michael Crawford notes the presence of Scripture impressed upon the hearts of those converted in the Cambuslang revival in the 1740s. See Michael J. Crawford, *Seasons of Grace: Colonial New England's Revival Tradition in Its British Context* (New York: Oxford University Press, 1991), 207-208.

Beloved saying, *Thou art all fair: there is no spot in thee.* [Song of Songs 4:7][13]

Interestingly, within the narrative Hall interpreted these words of Scripture as from God Himself.

Likewise, in her letter to John Wesley, Mrs. E. M—n recounts her experience of Perfection, marked three times by specific Scriptural passages: Romans 16:20, Revelation 3:8 and Psalm 42:1.[14] These Scriptures led up to her direct experience, and when questioning the validity of what happened, she is reassured by a direct encounter with God. She writes simply, "his Spirit bore witness, 'Thou *art* renewed.'"[15] Scripture played a significant role in her direct encounter with God that marked her experience of Christian Perfection.

It should also be noted that a direct experience of God need not be highly emotionally charged (what eighteenth-century critics of Methodism pejoratively called "enthusiasm"). In the accounts of George Clark and Bathsheba Hall, each specifically noted that the feeling was not rapturous, but a solid peace.[16] These steady accounts testify to the ability of the experience to be significant and transformative, even public, without being marked by a public display of emotion.

The middle of the narrative shows how in Perfection narratives, sanctification is affirmed as both slow growth and the divine encounter. These divine encounters marked a particular moment when God was present in response to faith; a specific time when God removed sin from the heart of believers. Additionally, the ability to recall and narrate this experience of being cleansed gave these early Methodists a particular narrative to communicate to others as they spoke about Christian Perfection.[17]

---

13. Hall, *Arminian Magazine*, 4:38. Also, Miss M. B. tells of a Mrs. Cayley who also received the words of Song of Songs 4:7 as she was cleansed. Miss M. B. to John Wesley, April 6, 1761, in *Arminian Magazine*, 4:278.

14. Romans 16:20: "And the God of peace shall bruise Satan under your feet shortly. The grace of our Lord Jesus Christ be with you. Amen." Revelation 3:8: "I know thy works: behold, I have set before thee an open door, and no man can shut it: for thou hast a little strength, and hast kept my word, and hast not denied my name." Psalm 42:1: "As the hart panteth after the water brooks, so panteth my soul after thee, O God." (KJV).

15. Mrs. E. M—n to John Wesley, Potto, March 11, 1762, in *Arminian Magazine*, 4:394.

16. Hall, *Arminian Magazine*, 4:38. Clark, *Arminian Magazine*, 6:245.

17. For example, George Clark shares his story at the Love-feast a week after the experience. Clark, *Arminian Magazine*, 6:246.

Without the story of the instantaneous event, the theological rhetoric of sanctification, such as the leaders of the movement taught, would not be nearly as memorable nor as personal.

End – Growth in Grace and Faithful Death

The end of the Perfection narrative is marked not by a static state of perfection, but by continued growth in grace. Aristotle delineates that the end of a narrative "is that which itself naturally occurs, whether necessarily or usually, after a preceding event, but need not be followed by anything else."[18] In the Perfection narrative, the end (that which "need not be followed by anything else") is marked by continued growth in grace. This continued growth is not unlike the apophatic tradition which asserts that there is always more to learn about God. The continued faithfulness and growth for the entire life of a Methodist was attested to by narratives of faithful death. The genre of these narratives, written by those who attended at the deathbed, could almost be classified as hagiography, since they contain glowing reports of saintliness. Yet, the testimony of those reporting the faithful death of their friend offers insight into the long lasting piety of those who claimed an experience of Perfection.

Two of the four narratives studied in this book include an extant narrative of faithful death witnessing to the continued growth in grace. The faithful death accounts of Sarah Crosby and William Hunter have already been explored showing the continued growth after their experience of Christian Perfection.[19] Furthermore, as seen in chapter eight, William Hunter's sermon illuminated continued growth after perfection. He notes, "when we enter into this great and glorious liberty, the Lord enlarges our capacity, and enables us to make swifter progress in the Divine life. ... We receive no new gift, but larger measures of the same love and grace, which prepared and fit us for eternal life."[20] Hunter describes here how the growth in grace is more of the same, not something new, and this aligns well with Aristotle's assertion that the end of a narrative is that which nothing follows. Methodist Perfection narratives are marked by an end that testifies to the continued growth in the same graces.

Similarly, the journal of George Clark illustrates the continuation of steady growth in grace after his Perfection narrative. Clark testified to an increase of the love he experienced, not something new, but more of the love he had already experienced. On December 11, 1763 he writes, "I found a purer love,

---

18. Aristotle, *Poetics*, 55.

19. See chapter six, page 62, and chapter eight, pages 90-91.

20. Letter from F. P. quoting William Hunter, October 6, 1797, in *Early Methodist Preachers*, 2:260.

and in a greater degree than ever, desiring his love more than any happiness to myself in heaven or earth; and being more abased than ever, by the great love of God to so vile a creature."[21] The story of Clark's life and spirituality continued after his Perfection narrative, as he encountered a purer form of God's love to a greater degree.

These elements — that is, the beginning, middle and end of the stories of Perfection — show the narrative arc of Perfection narratives in the life of the early Methodist. This arc includes the discovery of sin after conversion, both gradual and instantaneous sanctification received by faith, and also continued growth in grace after the experience of Christian Perfection. The study of Perfection, particularly through the narratives, highlights these aspects of the doctrine of Perfection.

---

21. Clark, *Arminian Magazine*, 6:352.

Conclusion

Unity and holiness are the two things I want among the Methodists
— John Wesley to John Fletcher, 1766[1]

God sent one of his dear people to see me, who had been long a witness of the Great Salvation. May that sacred day never be forgotten!
— Bathsheba Hall, 1768[2]

Examining the four case studies of Perfection narratives in this book demonstrates how the doctrine of Christian Perfection, while it was defined and taught by key leaders such as John and Charles Wesley, was spread among the early Methodist communities by narratives that embodied the doctrine. The narratives bore witness to an experience of God's love, as well as holiness of life, thus inspiring believers to seek out their own experience of Christian Perfection.

This study shows that narrative played a significant role in the transmission of the doctrine of Perfection. Narrative about the experience of Perfection was a source of inspiration to pursue holiness for those in the Methodist communities. By hearing the stories of how others had been cleansed from sin and had received pure love, the early Methodists caught a vision of holiness to which they aspired. In addition, hearing these narratives sometimes evoked a direct spiritual encounter between the listener and God, which encouraged the hope that the listener could also be transformed. Furthermore, it is seen how the chain of transmission by narrative continued through the Methodist structures: an experience is testified to at a class or band meeting, which then prompts others to seek holiness; this pursuit (or even attainment) of Perfection, was then shared through narrative with others in the community. Narrative evoked experience, which was declared in the form of narrative and the cycle began again.

Furthermore, these narratives help to nuance and embody the doctrine of Perfection. These narratives enrich the understanding of the doctrine by

---

1. John Wesley to John Fletcher, London, February 28, 1766, in *Letters*, 5:4.
2. Hall, *Arminian Magazine*, 4:36.

embodying the teaching of John and Charles Wesley, thus bringing forward aspects of the doctrine only seen when put into practice. Sarah Crosby's narrative embodies how the experience of Christian Perfection ebbs and flows over time. George Clark's narrative embodies the struggle with sin that remains after conversion. William Hunter's narrative embodies the ministry empowered by experiencing Christian Perfection. Finally, Bathsheba Hall embodies the ability to continue to grow and learn after such a significant spiritual experience. In these four narratives the struggle with sin is made real in the life of real people, and therefore, the joy of transformation and release from sin is also made real.

In summary, we have seen that in chapter six, lay preacher Sarah Crosby's story offers a complex narrative of Perfection in her letters and journals. Crosby entered into the Methodist community because she was seeking after the experience of love described as Christian Perfection by John and Charles Wesley. This seeking resulted in multiple intense encounters with God that have the characteristics of Perfection narratives of other Methodists. These experiences led to Crosby's freedom from inbred sin. Following these spiritual experiences her ministry among the Methodist communities involved both exhortation (formal sharing of her spiritual experiences) as well as informal sharing through leadership in classes and bands. Her journal entries embody the doctrine of Perfection by showing how her longing for Christian Perfection continued throughout her life, despite also experiencing significant freedom from sin.

In chapter seven, the life of George Clark demonstrates how narrative played a role in his spiritual storyline and in the spread of Christian Perfection among early Methodists. In Clark's journal are the stories of those that modelled Christian Perfection, as well as the influence of the lives of those who he wished not to imitate. The Perfectionist controversy and the separation of the London Methodist society impacted Clark's life and perspective on Methodist doctrine. Still, his Perfection narrative emerged from the controversy as a positive example, since, unlike those who sparked the controversy, he remained within the Methodist connexion. Furthermore, his journal was commended by Wesley when it was published in the *Arminian Magazine*. To use Wesley's appropriation of the parable, Clark is wheat harvested from among the tares.

The story of George Clark embodies the doctrine of Christian Perfection through both the struggle with sin after conversion and the transformation that is possible when freed from this struggle. The first eleven excerpts of Clark's journal illustrate well the daily struggle as ordinary elements of life (work and family) provoke sins such as anger and pride. Then suddenly, in the twelfth excerpt, there was release from that struggle through the experience of Christian Perfection. This release (and the transformation that followed) is all the more striking because of the honest struggle narrated previously in the journal. Clark enriches the understanding of the doctrine of Perfection through an embodied example of the struggle with sin after conversion and out of that struggle comes the embodiment of meaningful transformation.

In chapter eight, lay preacher William Hunter testified to his empowering experience of Christian Perfection in his letter to John Wesley. He received the doctrine through inspirational preaching and transmitted the doctrine to others in the same manner. Furthermore, he experienced God in an ecstatic way as he prayerfully sought after Christian Perfection. It was in direct response to his experience of Christian Perfection that he became an advocate for the doctrine when he became an itinerant preacher. Hunter's experience of Perfection embodies the doctrine by showing how the empowerment of an experience of Christian Perfection enabled Hunter to respond to the call of ministry. While his preaching contained the doctrine of Perfection, his life itself bore witness to holiness of life, which is seen in his faithful death narrative witnessing to the character of love that was cultivated by a life in pursuit of holiness.

In chapter nine, Bathsheba Hall's journal offers another witness to the experience of Christian Perfection. The journal documents Hall's Perfection narrative, a direct encounter with God through prayer. This experience was foundational as to how she reached out to others in prayer. Notably, in her journal she details how she shared the written testimony of her Experience and this sharing caused listeners to have their own direct experience with God. In addition to these encounters, the rest of the journal embodies the doctrine of Perfection by showing the growing maturity of faith that Hall experienced during the years after her Perfection experience: growth in spiritual self-understanding, growth in compassion for those around her and growth in perseverance as she patiently endured physical suffering. Hall's Perfection narrative, along with the rest of her spiritual journal, is an embodied witness to the doctrine of Christian Perfection which empowers the believer for ministry and dynamic growth in grace.

Where Do We Go from Here?

After hearing the narratives of perfection and examining how these narratives transmitted the doctrine, the question that remains: where do we go from here? What impact do these stories from more than two centuries ago have on people today? There are both implications for academic study, as well as implications for spiritual development for the body of Christ today, particularly those in the Wesleyan tradition.

Significance for Academic Inquiry

The study of Perfection narratives is significant in several ways for further academic studies by shedding light on the spirituality of the early Methodist people. First, the study of Perfection narratives enriches the understanding of the spiritual lifespan of the early Methodists by highlighting the pursuit of Perfection. Further to understanding the spiritual lifespan, these narratives push those using early Methodist spiritual writing as source material to consider the theological context of these narratives. Finally, the study of these Perfection narratives is significant for a growing understanding of the Perfectionist controversy in London in the 1760s.

The examination of Perfection narratives reveals that the shape of Methodist spirituality is formed by the transmission of spiritual narratives. Historian David Hempton notes that part of the goal of spiritual narrative is to tell a good story. He observes about Evangelical narratives that "they are meant to be good stories fit for the telling as well as honest accounts of states of mind."[3] The drama of the spiritual life of the Methodist is expressed through narrative. Examining Perfection narratives fills out the elements of the spiritual lifespan of Methodists to include seeking Christian Perfection as a distinct pursuit. This study shows how in addition to conversion narratives, early Methodists also narrated their experience of Perfection, which includes the discovery of inbred sin and a particular encounter with God which resulted in deep spiritual freedom.

Adding the Perfection narrative to conversion narratives and faithful death narratives, completes David Hempton's triptych of birth, life and death which is used to describe the three common Methodist narratives: conversion, Perfection and faithful death.[4] While Hempton draws attention to sanctification as the life pursuit of Methodists, his description focuses only on the pursuit of Perfection, and even suggests that it was often unrealistic to expect to attain Perfection.[5] It should be noted that not all Methodists had an experience of Perfection and thus could not include a Perfection narrative in their spiritual testimony. Yet, my study of the Perfection narratives in early British Methodism from those who did have the experience enriches that sample of narratives offered by Hempton

---

3. Hempton, *Empire of the Spirit*, 63.
4. Ibid., 60-68.
5. Ibid., 65.

in *Methodism: Empire of the Spirit*, which primarily consists of nineteenth century American Methodist narratives.[6]

The wider theological context for the narratives in this book is important. These narratives occurred in the context of real lives which also include experiences of conversion, deep spiritual friendships, as well as sacrifice and care for others. The theological revelations offered in these narratives also have implications for the whole spiritual lifespan. For example, the embodiment of the doctrine of Perfection seen in these narratives has revealed that the pursuit of Perfection involved the struggle with inbred sin, such as anger or pride. The pursuit of holiness evokes the hope of being rid of these deeply rooted sinful patterns of life. Thus, it is made clear that there are multiple waves of sorrow for sin. Before conversion, spiritual awakening evokes sorrow for sinful behaviour, while after conversion there is an additional wave of sorrow for the inbred sin which is deeply rooted in human fallenness. As a result different parts of the spiritual journey will look different in regards to sorrow for sin, and the hope of further holiness.

This theological context, which includes multiple experiences of sorrow for sin, is the necessary context for further work in the genre of Methodist spiritual narratives. Some of the recent studies of early British Methodism, which examine Methodist narratives from an interdisciplinary approach, do not display a robust theological understanding of Methodism, which has lead to misreading these narratives. For example, Phyllis Mack, in her study of British Methodism and emotion, takes note of the lack of attention to sanctification in male narratives.[7] She appears to draw the conclusion that men did not often experience Christian Perfection, in contrast to many sanctified women. While her effort to engage the distinctions between the male and female experience is valid, these conclusions make the contrast between gender too stark, when other explanations could be found. Consider that Mack's study of the male narratives draws from autobiographical letters which narrate the first wave of sorrow for sin, while the women's narratives are sourced from personal letters and diaries and focus on a later season in the spiritual life.[8] The

---

6. Hempton's excellent description of the Methodist ethos in *Empire of the Spirit* draws mainly on a different location and time period than my research, which could account for a slightly different expression of the Methodist spiritual lifespan.

7. Mack, *Heart Religion in the British Enlightenment*, 92, 131.

8. The sources used in Mack's study are not consistent between the genders. The main source for male narratives is the *Lives of the Early Methodist Preachers*, a collection of primarily solicited narratives. These solicited narratives often include the elements of upbringing, conversion and call into ministry. In contrast, for the women, Mack makes use of journals and personal letters. It is significant to note that

difference in genre of the source suggest that these other factors could explain the difference which Mack ascribes to gender. In contrast, in the sample of Perfection narratives for this book both male and female examples were explored in parallel genres. Granted, the first-hand male Perfection narratives were more difficult to locate than female narratives. Yet, George Clark, in particular, as a layman with a narrative of Perfection, draws attention to the similarities between men and women when comparing the Perfection narrative found in parallel sources such as journals.

Finally, the study of Perfection narratives provokes further study because it continues to enrich the understanding of the Perfectionist controversy in London in the 1760s. Both Gunter and Lloyd have offered new insight into the events of the Perfectionist controversy by examining manuscript evidence to enrich the account given by John Wesley.[9] These studies offer insights that suggest the situation was more complex than previously understood, yet their attention is focused only on the Perfection accounts which were dismissed as disreputable. It can be noted, from George Clark's narrative in particular (as a Perfection account that occurred in London during the Perfectionist controversy), that there is room for even more scholarship on the controversy. Indeed, it would be beneficial to study a wider sample of the narratives to illustrate the accepted experiences of Perfection which Wesley and others endorsed positively, as a contrast to the forms of Perfection from which Wesley distanced himself. The literature on the Perfectionist controversy would be enriched by taking seriously the observation by Gunter that there was an significant increase in the Perfection accounts in the early 1760s.[10] Not all of the people offering Perfection accounts were part of the following of Perfectionist preachers, Maxfield and Bell; many other stories remain untold.

Significance for Christian Spirituality Today

Further to the importance for academic study of Perfection narratives, there are implications for spirituality in the church today gleaned from the narratives found in this book. The transmission Christian Perfection through narrative forms provides an example how we may communicate spiritually significant themes. Furthermore, the spiritual journey of the early Methodists

---

journals and personal letters are a different genre from the solicited letter or the autobiography, since personal letters and journals are not initially intended for public consumption, even if later they are made public.

9. See chapter one, page 11, note 15.
10. Gunter, *Love Divine*, 204.

witnesses to the seriousness of sin in the life of believers even after conversion. Finally, these narratives draw attention to a key aspect of the Wesleyan tradition: seeking holiness. Each of these aspects of early Methodist spirituality offers encouragement to believers today.

The main argument of this book has been that the doctrine of Perfection passed from person to person through narrative. This idea has important implications for communication methods used in churches today. Employing narrative mediums alongside doctrinal education is effective for healthy spiritual growth. It was important for the early Methodists to hear the stories of their friends, leaders and even strangers as they sought to navigate the spiritual life to which they aspired. In addition, as seen in the narrative of George Clark, theological claims made through narrative must be supported by an appealing faith-filled life. The example offered by early Methodist history is that the power of narrative should not be underestimated when paired with the transformed lives to which the narratives witness.

The study of Perfection narratives is significant because it draws attention to the seriousness of sin and it also brings hope to human sinfulness, bearing witness to the possibility of real transformative change. The Perfection narratives in this study have illustrated the ability to be honest about the sin which is common to all of humanity. The seriousness of sin — as well as Wesley's two-fold description of outward and inward sin— largely has not been retained, even in the Wesleyan tradition. In these narratives I noticed a significant contrast between the eighteenth-century Methodist awareness of sin and the understanding of sin in our age. Many people today see sin simply as a finite list of prohibitions concerning certain external actions, but this is an inadequate definition of sin because a limited definition of sin also limits the scope of transformation that is possible in the Christian life.

By contrast, in the lives of the eighteenth-century Methodists, the awareness of inward sin, such as pride and anger, increased after conversion evoking a deep sense of the seriousness of sin. Rather than enslavement, this awareness of sin led to seeking the experience of Christian Perfection. These narratives suggest that even in our current culture of tolerance, we can name sin as sin and offer the hope of real change through the power of encountering God.

Finally, the implication for spiritual practice, particularly in the Wesleyan tradition, is that these narratives draw attention to holiness as an important part of the Wesleyan legacy. The narratives of Perfection in this study offer embodied examples of the serious pursuit of holiness: real transformation, increasing love, freedom from pride, anger and other besetting sins. These are aspects of Christian holiness not universally sought in twenty-first-century Evangelicalism.

The Wesleyan legacy of sanctification has been translated through the events of the nineteenth and twentieth centuries causing changes to our understanding of the doctrine, and as a result the distinctive Wesleyan doctrine of Christian Perfection is often lost. There are good reasons for setting aside the doctrine, for example if Perfection has turned into a moral perfectionism or spiritual elitism. But, true genuine spiritual maturity marked by holiness should still be a goal of all those who seek to know God more deeply. These narratives offer a positive examine of what holiness looks like, not simply a negative definition of what to avoid, thus the narratives of Christian Perfection cast a compelling vision of holiness.

To conclude: this study has shown how the doctrine of Christian Perfection in early British Methodism, taught by John and Charles Wesley, was significantly transmitted through narratives of the experience of Perfection. The narratives of a variety of early Methodists, particularly the four sampled in this book, embody the doctrine of perfection through testimony and holiness of life, illuminating nuances of the doctrine and inspiring others to pursue their own experience of Christian Perfection.

The Sources

Sarah Crosby

The available literary sources penned by Sarah Crosby are her journal and some of the letters she exchanged with fellow Methodists, including her correspondence with John Wesley. A substantial quantity of these sources is preserved in a collection of excerpts from her journal, published in the *Methodist Magazine* in 1806 as a tribute. The publication came two years after her death in 1804.[1] This memoir was republished twenty-two years later, collated with additional correspondence and journal entries, as part of Zachariah Taft's collection of narratives in support of Methodist women preachers.[2] In addition to the published sources, a letterbook (containing some of the above published items, and other unpublished items) is housed at Duke University. Crosby's life and narrative comes alive in this letterbook where she copied letters which she received and wrote, and she used part of the book as a journal — such everyday uses for a blank book.[3]

In addition to the sources penned by Crosby, there are references to her by those she ministered to in the Methodist community, and there is mention of her in John Wesley's diary.[4] In both the *Methodist Magazine* excerpts and Taft's profile in *Holy Women,* Crosby's story concludes with a letter from her friend, Anne Tripp, giving the account of Crosby's faithful death.[5] These sources,

---

1. Sarah Crosby, "The Grace of God Manifested, In an Account of Mrs. Crosby, of Leeds," Methodist Magazine 29 (1806): 418-423, 465-473, 517-521, 563-568, 610-617. The *Methodist Magazine* is the continuation of the *Arminian Magazine*.

2. Crosby, *Holy Women*, 2:23-114.

3. Frank Baker writes about the letterbook and Crosby in Baker, "John Wesley and Sarah Crosby," 76-82. I had the opportunity to examine the letterbook at Duke University, June 17, 2009.

4. John Wesley, July 22, 1789, *Journal and Diaries VII (1787-1791)*, ed. W. Reginald Ward and Richard P. Heitzenrater, vol. 24 of *The Bicentennial Edition of the Works of John Wesley* (Nashville: Abingdon Press, 1997), 521. This diary entry simply notes that Wesley sat and read letters with S. Crosby, among others. Other Methodists mention Sarah Crosby; for example, in her life story Mary Holder gives testimony to the impact of Sarah Crosby on her community, noting that "their labours *publicly* and *privately* were blest in town and country to numbers of precious souls." And that Crosby "was a pattern of holiness in all manner of conversation. Her life and labours of love were of great use to my soul and *I bless God that I ever saw her.*" Mary Holder, *Holy Women*, 1:104.

5. Letter from Anne Tripp, in *Holy Women*, 2:112-115. Letter from Anne Tripp, in *Methodist Magazine*, 29 (1806) 615-617.

taken together, give a significant picture of the spirituality of Sarah Crosby, yet there has been little scholarly attention given to Crosby beyond her role in challenging the social boundaries forbidding women to preach.[6]

George Clark

The sources of information regarding the life of George Clark are limited. There are the journal extracts published in the *Arminian Magazine* in 1782 and 1783 under the name Mr. G— C—. Despite the anonymity offered by Wesley publishing the journal without the full name, the journal references a conversation where the author's friend, Thomas Walsh, calls him George.[7] Additionally, a letter from the same author is published in the *Arminian Magazine* in 1787 as from Mr. G. Clark, thus putting the names together Mr. G. C. is revealed as George Clark.[8]

Another resource in the *Arminian Magazine* which appears to be from Clark is a short theological treatise on sanctification. This treatise by Mr. G. C. reflects theologically on the Perfectionist controversy in London in the 1760s.[9] In addition to the sources in the *Arminian Magazine*, there are two references to Clark in John Wesley's collected letters. First, a letter is addressed to a guest in Clark's house.[10] Second, there is a letter from Wesley to Mary Bosanquet who mentions "honest George Clark."[11] Additionally, a folder of manuscript letters from George Clark to Mary (Bosanquet) Fletcher is an interesting, but as yet untapped resource for more information on Clark's spiritual narrative.[12] The final artifact regarding this early Methodist man is a

---

6. For a bibliography including scholarly references to Sarah Crosby, see appendix in Paul Wesley Chilcote, *John Wesley and the Women Preachers of Early Methodism* (Metuchen, NJ: The American Theological Library Association, 1991) 255-259. An exception to the attention only on Crosby's role as preacher is the dissertation by Irelan which examines practical divinity and uses Crosby's journal as source material. Rebecca Jane Irelan, "A Little Experiment in Pragmatic Divinity: Charles Sanders Peirce and the Women of Early Methodism Socialize the Subject of John Wesley's Doctrine of Sanctification," (PhD diss., Graduate Theological Union, 2008).

7. Clark, *Arminian Magazine*, 6:19.

8. Clark to Wesley, in *Arminian Magazine* 10:103-105. The letter indicates it is from the same author as the journal because it mentions a Perfection experience on the same day as noted in the journal.

9. Clark, *Arminian Magazine*, 13:42-45. For more on the Perfectionist controversy, see chapter one, pages 11-12.

10. John Wesley to Jonah Freeman, December 20, 1762, in *Letters*, 4:197.

11. John Wesley to Mary Bosanquet, in *Letters*, 7:43.

12. The John Rylands University archives, MAM/FL/2.4. I accessed this folder of manuscript letters through the online archival notes where the presence of spiritual reflection is noted but the content of the

gravestone. George John Stevenson wrote a short biography of George Clark when he examined the gravestones at City Road Chapel in London. The gravestone records his death date as May 14, 1797 at age 86.[13]

William Hunter

The story of William Hunter is among the spiritual testimonies printed in the *Arminian Magazine* by John Wesley. His witness to both conversion and Perfection was offered to the people who heard Hunter preach, but the readership of the *Arminian Magazine* provided a wider audience for his narrative.[14] Two letters were published in the *Arminian Magazine*, accompanied by a image of Hunter in the form of a woodcutting. The letters were written to John Wesley by Hunter and they form the core of the sources for the spiritual life of this lay preacher. The letters are simple and honest. Hunter mentions in his first letter that his story was solicited by Wesley and that he had not kept notes on his spiritual life. In his second letter he reflects on his experience of being saved from inbred sin, offering to "simply relate what I know of the dealings of God with me in this respect."[15] Yet, ever the preacher, he does offer some interpretation, not solely his story. Still, the power behind his exhortation to holiness is his narrative of experiencing Christian Perfection.

The two letters found in the *Arminian Magazine* were reprinted in *The Lives of Early Methodist Lay Preachers*, with the addition of an account of Hunter's faithful death and a letter of testimony about Hunter written by a friend.[16] There also is evidence of Hunter in lists of lay preachers in the minutes of the Methodist conferences and John Wesley mentions him in his journal a few times.[17]

---

reflections are not reported. Manuscript research is outside the scope of this thesis which is limited to published resources. Accessed at http://archives.li.man.ac.uk/ead/html/gb135mam-fl-1-p16.shtml. Phyllis Mack quotes from one of the archival letters in her book, *Heart Religion in the British Enlightenment: Gender and Emotion in Early Methodism* (Cambridge: Cambridge University Press, 2008), 135.

13. George John Stevenson, *City Chapel Road, London, and its Associations, Historical, Biographical, and Memorial* (London: George J. Stevenson, 1872), 506-507.

14. Hunter to Wesley, August 18, 29, 1779, in *Arminian Magazine*, 2:589-598.

15. Hunter to Wesley, August 29, 1779, in *Early Methodist Preachers*, 2:246.

16. Ibid., 2:240-261.

17. Mentions of Hunter in other sources include: Wesley, June 5, 1772, *Journals and Diaries V*, eds. Ward, Heitzenrater (Nashville: Abingdon, 1993), 22:331-333, 335. A portion of the account recorded in the journal is also found in Wesley, "Short History of People Called Methodists," in *The Methodist Societies*, ed. Davies, vol. 9 of *Works* 9:496-497. John Wesley to Christopher Hopper, Rotherham, July 25, 1774, in *Letters*, 6:103. Also a passing mention of William Hunter in Letters, 6:141. The Conference

Bathsheba Hall

The source for Bathsheba Hall's life is her journal excerpted in the *Arminian Magazine* from January through July in 1781, beginning only a few months after her death.[18] Additionally, John Wesley mentions Hall and her husband in his journal as local saints while passing through Bristol in September 1779.[19] Also of note is that a short biography and a prayer from Bathsheba Hall is included in Paul Wesley Chilcote's *Early Methodist Spirituality* taken from the *Arminian Magazine* excerpts.[20] Interestingly, Z. Taft includes a biography of a different Bathsheba Hall, a preacher later in the movement, in his collection, *Holy Women*.

---

minutes for 1791 state that William Hunter was a preacher stationed at Yarm. John Wesley, *Minutes of several Conversations between Preachers Late in Connection with the Rev. Mr. Wesley* (London, 1791), 10. This confirms what Hunter notes in his letter that he has been stationed at Yarm, Hunter to Wesley, Aug 18, 1779, in *Early Methodist Preachers*, 2:244. The "Deed of Declaration" (signed February 28, 1784) lists "William Hunter of Berwick-upon-Tweed" as present to witness. John Wesley, *The Journal of the Rev. John Wesley, A.M. Sometime Fellow of Lincoln College, Oxford. Enlarged from Original Mss., with notes from unpublished diaries, annotations, maps, and illustrations*, ed. Nehemiah Curnock (London: Epworth, 1938), 8:338.

18. Hall, *Arminian Magazine*, 4:35-40, 94-97, 148-152, 195-198, 256-259, 309-311, 372-376.
19. Wesley, Sept 23, 1779, *Journal and Diaries VI*, in *Works*, 23:149.
20. Chilcote, *Early Methodist Spirituality*, 226.

Bibliography

Primary Sources

Clark, George. "Thoughts on the Work of Sanctification." In *The Arminian Magazine: Consisting of Extracts and Original Treatises on Universal Redemption*, 13 (1790): 42-45.

———. "An Extract from the Journal of Mr. G— C—." In *The Arminian Magazine: Consisting of Extracts and Original Treatises on Universal Redemption*, 5 (1782): 298-301, 351-355, 404-408, 465-468, 519-524, 575-580, 639-641; 6 (1783): 19-22, 73-76, 125-127, 186-189, 244-246, 299-302, 352-355, 407-410, 464-468.

Chilcote, Paul Wesley, ed. *Early Methodist Spirituality: Selected Women's Writings*. Nashville: Kingswood, 2007.

Crosby, Sarah. "The Grace of God Manifested, In an Account of Mrs. Crosby, of Leeds." In *Methodist Magazine* 29 (1806): 418-423, 465-473, 517-521, 563-568, 610-617.

Fletcher, Mary. *The Life of Mrs. Mary Fletcher*. Edited by Henry Moore. New York: Soule & Mason, 1818.

Gilbert, Ann. "The Experience of Mrs. Ann Gilbert, of Gwinear in Cornwall." In *Arminian Magazine*, 18 (1795): 42-46.

Hall, Bathsheba. "An Extract from the Diary of Mrs. Bathsheba Hall." In *Arminian Magazine*, 4 (1781): 35-40, 94-97, 148-152, 195-198, 256-259, 309-311, 372-376.

Hunter, William. William Hunter to John Wesley. In *The Lives of Early Methodist Preachers: Chiefly Written by Themselves*. Edited by Thomas Jackson, 3rd ed. Vol. 2, 240-261. London: Wesleyan Conference Office, 1878.

Jackson, Thomas, ed. *The Lives of Early Methodist Preachers Chiefly Written by Themselves*. 3rd ed. 6 vols. London: Wesleyan Conference Office, 1878.

Mortimer, E. Mrs. E. Mortimer to the editor of the Methodist Magazine, Islington, January 7, 1806, in *Methodist Magazine*, 29 (1806): 418.

Rogers, Hester Ann. *An Account of the Experience of Mrs. H. A. Rogers*. London: T. Cordeux, 1818.

Taft, Z. *Biographical Sketches of the Lives and Public Ministry of Various Holy Women, whose eminent usefulness and successful labours in the Church of Christ, have entitled them to be enrolled among the great benefactors of mankind: In which are included several letters from the Rev. J. Wesley never before published*. 2 vol. London, 1825.

Tripp, Anne. Letter from Anne Tripp, in *Methodist Magazine*, 29 (1806): 615-617.

Wesley, Charles. *The Journal of The Rev. Charles Wesley, M.A.* Edited by Thomas Jackson. 2 vols. Grand Rapids: Baker, 1980.

———. *The Manuscript Journal of the Reverend Charles Wesley, M.A.* Edited by S T Kimbrough, Jr. and Kenneth G. C. Newport. Nashville: Kingswood Books, 2008.

Wesley, John. *A Plain Account of Christian Perfection, as believed and taught by the Rev. Mr. John Wesley, from the year 1725 to the year 1777*. 6th ed. London, 1789.

———. *The Arminian Magazine: Consisting of Extracts and Original Treatises on Universal Redemption*, vol. 1-14. London, 1778-1791.

———. *The Bicentennial Edition of The Works of John Wesley*. Edited by Frank Baker and Richard P. Heitzenrater. Nashville: Abingdon Press, 1976-.

———. "Cautions and Directions Given to the Greatest Professors in the Methodist Societies," in *John Wesley*. Edited by Albert C. Outler. 298-305. New York: Oxford University Press, 1964.

———. *The Journal of the Rev. John Wesley, A.M. Sometime Fellow of Lincoln College, Oxford. Enlarged from Original Mss., with notes from unpublished diaries, annotations, maps, and illustrations*. Edited by Nehemiah Curnock. London: Epworth Press, 1938.

———. *The Letters of the Rev. John Wesley, A.M.* Edited by John Telford. 8 vols. London: Epworth Press, 1931.

Wesleyan Methodist Church Conference. *Minutes of several conversations, between the Rev. John Wesley, A.M. and the preachers in connection with him. Containing the form of discipline established among the preachers and people in the Methodist societies*. London, 1779 [1797].

Secondary Sources

Albin, Thomas R. "An Empirical Study of Early Methodist Spirituality." In *Wesleyan Theology Today: A Bicentennial Theological Consultation*. Edited by Theodore Runyon. 275-290. Nashville: Kingswood Books, 1985.

———. "'Inwardly Persuaded': Religion of the Heart in Early British Methodism." In *"Heart Religion" in the Methodist Tradition and Related Movements*. Edited by Richard B. Steele. Pietist and Wesleyan Studies 12. 33-66. Lanham, MD: Scarecrow Press, 2001.

Aristotle. *Poetics*. Edited and translated by Stephen Halliwell. Loeb Classical Library. Cambridge, MA: Harvard University Press, 1995.

Baker, Frank. *Charles Wesley: As Revealed by His Letters*. Revised edition. Madison, NJ: The Charles Wesley Society, 1995.

———. "John Wesley and Sarah Crosby." *Proceedings of the Wesley Historical Society* 27 no. 4 (Dec 1949): 76-82.

Brown, Earl Kent. *Women of Mr. Wesley's Methodism*. New York: Edwin Mellen Press, 1983.

Chilcote, Paul Wesley. *John Wesley and the Women Preachers of Early Methodism*. Metuchen, NJ: The American Theological Library Association, 1991.

Cox, Leo George. *John Wesley's Concept of Perfection*. Kansas City, Missouri: Beacon Hill Press, 1964.

Crawford, Michael J. *Seasons of Grace: Colonial New England's Revival Tradition in Its British Context*. New York: Oxford University Press, 1991.

Crites, Stephen. "The Narrative Quality of Experience" *Journal of the American Academy of Religion* 39 no. 3 (Sep 1971): 291-311.

Curtis, O. A. *The Christian Faith*. New York: The Methodist Book Concern, 1905.

Dreyer, Frederick. *The Genesis of Methodism*. Bethlehem: Lehigh University Press, 1999.

Flew, R. Newton. "Methodism." In *The Idea of Perfection in Christian Theology: An Historical Study of the Christian Ideal for the Present Life*. 313-341. Oxford: Clarendon Press, 1934. Reprinted 1968.

Goodwin, Charles H. "Setting Perfection too High: John Wesley's Changing Attitudes Toward the 'London Blessing'." *Methodist History* 36, no. 2 (January 1998): 86-96.

Gunter, W. Stephen. *The Limits of 'Love Divine.'* Nashville: Kingswood Books, 1989.

Heitzenrater, Richard P. "Great Expectations: Aldersgate and the Evidences of Genuine Christianity." In *Aldersgate Reconsidered*. Edited by Randy L. Maddox. 49-91. Nashville: Kingswood, 1990.

———. *Wesley and the People Called Methodists*. Nashville: Abingdon Press, 1995.

Hempton, David. *Methodism: Empire of the Spirit*. New Haven: Yale University Press, 2005.

Hindmarsh, Bruce. *The Evangelical Conversion Narrative: Spiritual Autobiography in Early Modern England*. Oxford: Oxford University Press, 2005.

Lindström, Harald. *Wesley and Sanctification: A study in the doctrine of salvation*. London: Epworth, 1946.

Lloyd, Gareth. "'A Cloud of Perfect Witnesses': John Wesley and the London Disturbances 1760-1763." *The Asbury Theological Journal* vol. 56 no. 2 – vol. 57, no 1. (2001-2002): 117-136.

———. *Charles Wesley and the Struggle for Methodist Identity*. Oxford: Oxford University Press, 2007.

Mack, Phyllis. *Heart Religion in the British Enlightenment: Gender and Emotion in Early Methodism*. Cambridge: Cambridge University Press, 2008.

Maddox, Randy L. *Responsible Grace: John Wesley's Practical Theology*. Nashville: Kingwood, 1994.

———. "Reconnecting the Means to the End: A Wesleyan Prescription for the Holiness Movement." *Wesleyan Theological Journal* 33 no. 2 (1998): 29-66.

Moore, D. Marselle. "Development in Wesley's Thought on Sanctification and Perfection." *Wesleyan Theological Journal* 2 no 2 (1985): 29-53.

Outler, Albert Cook. "John Wesley: Folk-theologian." *Theology Today* 34, no. 2 (July 1, 1977): 150-160.

Niebuhr, H. Richard. *The Meaning of Revelation*. New York: MacMillian, 1941.

Rack, Henry D. *Reasonable Enthusiast: John Wesley and the Rise of Methodism*. 3rd ed. London: Epworth, 2002.

Sangster, W. E. *The Path to Perfection: An Examination and Restatement of John Wesley's Doctrine of Christian Perfection*. London: Epworth Press, 1957.

Stevenson, George John. *City Chapel Road, London, and its Associations, Historical, Biographical, and Memorial.* George J. Stevenson, 1872. 506-507.

Tyson, John R. *Charles Wesley on Sanctification: A Biographical and Theological Study.* Grand Rapids: Francis Asbury Press, 1986.

———. *Assist Me to Proclaim: The Life and Hymns of Charles Wesley.* Grand Rapids: Eerdmans, 2007.

Dissertations

Irelan, Rebecca Jane. "A Little Experiment in Pragmatic Divinity: Charles Sanders Peirce and the Women of Early Methodism Socialize the Subject of John Wesley's Doctrine of Sanctification." PhD diss., Graduate Theological Union, 2008.

Loving, Gregory. "Narrative and Power Toward a Theology of the Overdog." PhD. diss., Graduate Theological Union, 2000.

Vinskie, Erica L. "Becoming Catholic: Story, Sacrament, Conversion and the Emergence of Faith in Postconciliar Autobiographies." M.A. Thesis, Temple University, 2011.